GENRE · TROPE · GENDER

CRITICAL ESSAYS BY

GENRE

NORTHROP FRYE,

·TROPE·

LINDA HUTCHEON,

GENDER

AND SHIRLEY NEUMAN

Published by Carleton University Press

ISBN 0-88629-189-5 (paperback)
Printed and bound in Canada

Canadian Cataloguing in Publication Data

Main entry under title:
  Genre, trope, gender: critical essays

Contents: Frye, Northrop. Henry James and the comedy of the occult. — Hutcheon, Linda. The power of postmodern irony. — Neuman, Shirley. Autobiography, mothers' bodies, the reproduction of mothering.

Includes index.

ISBN 0-88629-189-5 (pbk.)

  1. Literature—History and criticism. I. Rutland, Barry II. Frye, Northrop, 1912-1991. Henry James and the comedy of the occult. III. Hutcheon, Linda, 1947-   . The power of postmodern irony. IV. Neuman, Shirley, 1946-   . Autobiography, mothers' bodies, the reproduction of mothering.

PN85. G46 1992   809   C92-090510–2

Cover Design: Colton Temple Design

Typeset in 10.5/13.5 Berkeley by
Nancy Poirier Type Services Ltd., Ottawa.

Acknowledgements

Carleton University Press gratefully acknowledges the support extended to its publishing programme by the Canada Council and the Ontario Arts Council.

The Press would also like to thank the Department of Canadian Heritage, Government of Canada, and the Governement of Ontario through the Ministry of Culture, Tourism and Recreation, for their assistance.

THE MUNRO BEATTIE LECTURES
1989•1990•1991

GENRE · TROPE · GENDER

CRITICAL ESSAYS

BY

NORTHROP FRYE

LINDA HUTCHEON

SHIRLEY NEUMAN

EDITED BY BARRY RUTLAND

CARLETON UNIVERSITY PRESS
FOR
THE DEPARTMENT OF ENGLISH
CARLETON UNIVERSITY
OTTAWA, CANADA

CONTENTS

Foreword

This volume includes the texts of three public lectures by eminent literary scholars delivered at Carleton University in honour of a man who, in a working life that spans more than a half century, has contributed much to the advancement of English studies in Canada. Alexander Munro Beattie was one of the original faculty members of Carleton University and founder of its Department of English. In 1942 he joined a group of teachers under the leadership of that inveterate founder of institutions of higher learning, Henry Marshall Tory, to offer opportunities to the many men and women who had either interrupted or postponed their university education to come to Ottawa as public servants in wartime. From a small number of basic arts and science courses given in church halls and high school class rooms, Carleton College developed into a major university, renowned internationally in many fields. Munro Beattie was at the heart of this process of growth and fulfilment, presiding over the development of the English department in particular but contributing to all aspects of institutional evolution. When he stepped down from the chair in 1968, the department's teaching staff exceeded the entire faculty at the time Carleton first opened its doors and was contributing to all branches of English studies—undergraduate, graduate, and extension teaching, bibliographical, historical, and critical scholarship, and service to disciplinary organizations. Munro Beattie, one of the original contributors to *A Literary History of Canada*, has a further claim to esteem as a founder of the study of Canadian literature as an academic discipline. The Carleton English Department was among the first to make knowledge of our literature a condition of the B.A. degree and to emphasize it in graduate research.

The lecture series was inaugurated in 1986 by Eli Mandel of York University. The 1987 and 1988 lectures were given respectively by Paul Fussell of the University of Pennsylvania and Claude Bissell of the University of Toronto, a former president of Carleton. Their lectures have been published in pamphlet form, edited by R.H. MacDonald (see below), and are available through the university book store. The department decided to combine the 1989, 1990, and 1991 lectures in a single volume to commemorate the fiftieth anniversary of the founding of Carleton and, in particular, to honour Munro Beattie's contribution to the birth and growth of the university.

* * * * * * * * * * * * *

That the authors of these papers are three outstanding figures of the present and immediately previous generations in literary studies in Canada, and that they deal with aspects of three of the major categories in such studies today, is a happy accident. The development of theories of genre, trope, and gender that take into account the revolutions of the twentieth century in our conception of human cognition, symbolic activities, and ontology are central to current research and debate, and the investigation of literary texts in terms of these theories are central to teaching and critical writing. These papers by Northrop Frye, Linda Hutcheon, and Shirley Neuman are points on the trajectory of theoretical development and critical application during the past thirty-five years. With *Anatomy of Criticism*, Northrop Frye assumed a leading role in inaugurating the contemporary "Age of Theory" in the study of literature. We may have forgotten the enormous impact of that book when it first appeared in 1957. For many Canadian scholars it was Frye rather than European theorists who opened a wider view of what constituted literary merit and significant critical problems than those accomodated by New Criticism and the old historicism. The other two contributors, while not disciples of Frye, are beneficiaries of his achievement. Linda Hutcheon of the University of Toronto is currently Canada's leading figure in the international development of cultural theory through her impressive series of books and articles on postmodernism. Shirley Neuman of the University of Alberta has emerged as a major scholar in the field of life writing and the role of literature in the formation of subjectivities. The following brief introductory remarks will try to situate each essay within the author's general intellectual project and the context of literary studies at the present time.

Northrop Frye is above all a theoretician of genre: *Anatomy of Criticism* is a mapping of the literary field as a complex system of kinds that relate to one another in terms of rhetorical and stylistic categories. Frye's Myth Criticism is out of fashion now and its historical importance in the evolution of a "scientific" criticism that sought to ground itself in its object of study, literature, rather than in extraneous matters, and at the same time regarded its activities as autonomous of that object and valid in their own right, is insufficiently appreciated. From a poststructuralist perspective *Anatomy of Criticism*, with its elaborate scheme that purports to account for every possible variety of verbal art, tends to look like the work of one of the obsessive cranks Frye speaks of in his essay. Of course, Frye built his system on the body of received literary theoretical notions from Aristotle to T.S. Eliot without the benefit of the innovations in the concepts of language, discourse, and text initiated by Saussure and the Russian Formalists and reworked during the very years in which he was writing *Anatomy* by Lévi-Strauss and his structuralist disciples. For many younger scholars, for whom semiotics, deconstruction, and psychoanalysis are the compelling interpretants of literature, Frye's theory must seem like the monuments of the Maya, surprising remains of a people with a neolithic economy, achieved independently of the Old World—impressive, but not of our tradition. Frye's genre categories, however, are far from cranky: the four mythoi and their twenty-four phases constitute a "high resolution" topography of literary kinds that enables specificity of categorization and evaluation of texts. It is rather like D'Arcy Thompson's taxonomy of the animal kingdom in terms of subtle gradations of morphological difference that elicit relations among known species and permits interpolation and extrapolation to species unknown or that might evolve in the future (Thompson 1917). Frye had reason to claim scientific status for his theory.

In "Henry James and the Comedy of the Occult," possibly the last major statement to be published after his death, Frye brings his theory to bear, lightly, on the work of a major novelist, an area of literature under-represented in his practical criticism, which deals largely with poetry. The essay, judging from the evidence it provides, outlines a reading of James's fiction which began in Frye's student days and extended virtually to the end of his life. As Frye notes in his opening paragraph, he came to appreciate James rather late in his education. That he made up for this is evident in the fact that James rates sixteen entries in the index to *Anatomy*, the same number as Dickens, ahead of Hawthorne and Hardy—fifteen each—exceeded only by Fielding with seventeen. In the essay here, Frye cites forty titles from James's oeuvre. His entry point to James, he tells us, was the chance purchase of second-hand copies of two unfinished novels, *The Ivory Tower* and *The Sense of the Past*. It is perhaps typical of Frye to be attracted by a certain marginality: witness his fascination with William Blake, a problematic poet, marginal to the canon—until the publication of *Fearful Symmetry* (1947)—the dissection of whose work resulted in *Anatomy*. In the case of Henry James, the attraction was to an unfinished work accompanied by extensive authorial notes, its anatomy helplessly exposed to the critic's scrutiny. *The Sense of the Past* became Frye's map for reading the entire corpus of James's fiction. As he remarks toward the end of his essay, it is for him "a kind of abstract model of the type of story [James] had been telling all his life." This is because of the *occult* nature of the work. Frye points out that the conventions of the Victorian ghost story are pervasive to James's fiction. The most haunted of them, *The Turn of the Screw*, is a tale told about the fire at Christmas in the tradition of Dickens; however, while we cannot be sure what it is that the governess-narrator sees or thinks she sees, belief in the objective existence of spirits is not the issue. In two other well-known stories in which ghost story conventions are patent, *The Beast in the Jungle* and *The Sacred Fount*, paranoid fear and obsessive imagination are the conjurers of occult presences in the mind. But James's fiction in general tends to deal with the surprising irruption of the unseen or, rather, the unforeseen as alternative meanings into the world of the conventional and supposedly settled. In other words, the ghost story is a latent structural model. Thus Frye does here what he does so frequently in *Anatomy* and elsewhere, treat a received genre concept as malleable clay to be molded to fit the exingencies of actual texts.

In Frye's estimation, Henry James is not a realist or naturalist in the nineteenth century "low mimetic" tradition—more precisely, his social realism is in tension with this other factor which Frye terms the occult. Frye sees the quest for "intensity of experience" as the abiding project of James's fiction, and the potential for experience as always exceeding what can be named or realized. The occult provided James with a device for presenting this irreducible duality in narrative form. Generically, the bulk of James's fiction belongs to Frye's category of ironic comedy, the "first phase" of the comic mode. In what is generally understood by the term comedy, "third phase" comedy in Frye's scheme, the obstruction of a "blocking humor"—a heavy father or similar type—is overcome, permitting the young lovers to marry and live fruitfully. In ironic variants, "the humor is ... likely to retain ... ascendancy...." This tends to be very much the case with James. The paradigm of the James novel is the "international situation", the encounter of ardent (and usually rich) Americans with European civilization. The Americans seek an intensity of experience that they hope Europe can provide. The quest generally fails or concludes equivocally—consider the destinies of Lambert Strether, Maggie Verver, and Millie Theale from the great late novels, or of Isabel Archer in the best known. Frye draws our attention to a peculiarly Jamesian version of the blocking humor, the individual in the grips of an obsessive theory of life, or blindly devoted to a fetish-object. A theory is a "sighting" and James's obsessive theorists think they see what others do not or cannot, to their own misery and that of those around them. Such fiction cannot be read according to the canons of naturalism; it stages another scene. Frye's treatment of James tends to place that writer among the modernists—indeed, if we apply Frye's theory to developments that were just beginning to become apparent in fiction at the time of the publication of *Anatomy*, James frequently anticipates postmodernist practice in his subversion of realist representational norms and the value assumptions they serve.

Questions of genre are at the forefront of contemporary literary studies because, as theoreticians such as Mikhail Bakhtin teach us, the various genres are templates that enable discourses to be produced as texts: as language can be realized only in specific orders of discourse, with their parameters of obligation and prohibition (this must be said, that may not be said), so discourse must be embodied in one or other appropriate genre with its facilitations and constraints. Genres are the highest units of symbolic selection and combination susceptible to formalization. The dynamic behind the generic modelling of discourse derives from the tropes, conceived not or not simply as a system of classification, a rule of ornament, or a recipe for persuasion, but as constituting a fundamental cognitive faculty of the mind. Frye implicitly recognizes rhetoric in these terms in establishing relations of interdependency between tropes and genres. He designates irony as a generic mode in itself in *Anatomy* but specifies it in terms of a familiar genre, satire. It is precisely the trope irony that links satire with its immediate neighbour in the cycle of modes and phases, ironic comedy. Thus, as Frye's work adumbrates current thought concerning genre, so it does with trope. Hayden White, working out of Giambattista Vico and Kenneth Burke (White 1978), has produced a cyclic tropological scheme that compares interestingly with Frye's cycle of generic modes. White sees the ironic mode as registering the breakdown of discursive certainty, an opening into what may be termed, in Bakhtinian vocabulary, the generative potentialities of carnival.

Postmodernism seems to be governed by irony and to engage in carnival's dehierarchizing of discourses. The postmodern is notoriously difficult to characterize, but there appears to be a general agreement that it is a response to the dissolution of the modernist cultural order, grounded in the utopian faith of both the Enlightment and its Romantic Other in ineluctable material progress and spiritual emancipation (see Lyotard 1984). Irony is the "master trope," to use White's phrase out of Burke, of the carnivalesque passage from a decaying cultural paradigm to a new. This is the territory that Linda Hutcheon has been exploring over the past dozen years. Hutcheon has attacked the problem of the postmodern along a number of intersecting axes: the problematics of metanarrative (1984), parody (1985), irony (1991), and historical context (1988 a,b), defining a field of objects and developing a theory to account for them. Like Frye, she grounds her theory in textual practices, in her case those of late twentieth century writers and visual artists, with the aim of producing "a flexible conceptual structure which could at once constitute and contain postmodern culture and our discourses both about it and adjacent to it." (Hutcheon 1988: ix) Hutcheon has yet to publish a *Rhetoric of Postmodernism* and the larger study of irony promised in the preface to *Splitting Images: Contemporary Canadian Ironies* may be that book. In a sense, the essay printed here, a version of the last chapter of *Splitting Images*, is an outline for it. Throughout her work, Hutcheon in effect historicizes and problematizes the idea of irony encountered in Frye and other founders of contemporary literary theory. While the "master tropes"—White's list includes irony, metaphor, metonymy, and synecdoche—may be a set of hard-wired neural processes and, as such, constitute a limit to human cognition, their functions and effects vary in relation to the historical situation of individuals and groups. This is the heart of Linda Hutcheon's argument in "The Power of Postmodern Irony." Frye tends to see irony in traditional terms as the trope of satire, and satire as centred in ethical norms. Hutcheon, drawing on the work of Alan Wilde, notes the limitations of this "premodernist" Augustan notion of irony and compares it with Romantic irony, serving the ethos of the poet-ironist, and modernist irony as theorized by the New Critics, that aims for balanced amibiguity of statement. Postmodern irony differs from all of these in being "suspensive," unwilling to take sides. Irony, one might say, is an ethical trope that displays the disparity between appearance and reality, what is acknowledged and what is repressed. Hutcheon sees postmodern irony as aimed at maintaining openings to semantic potentiality against monologic closure. Her chief anatagonists in this essay are the Marxist literary theoreticians, represented by Fredric Jameson and Terry Eagleton, who regard postmodern culture as late capitalism's opium of the masses, superficially antagonistic to consumerism and neo-conservatism while complicit with them in serving to construct subjectivities compliant with their project, a dressed down successor to the old High Culture humanism of Matthew Arnold and F.R. Leavis. In opposition to this view, Hutcheon, as critical of the exploitative tendencies of late capitalist marketplace culture as Eagleton or Jameson, argues that postmodern art, through deployment of deconstructive irony within the culture it critiques, exposes false consciousness and bad faith. Postmodern irony does not promote veridical norms or supply programs for action: it maintains fluidity of consciousness where all norms have been revealed as illusions and all programs have failed, but where new meaning is always potentially available through inversions and recombinations—radical "tropings"—of existing discourses. Its political power is a function of its ethical practice.

Contemporary theory is preoccupied with the role of literature and other cultural practices in the construction of individuals as subjects, that is, selves that bear culture within them and reproduce it as nature. Investigation of gender is basic to that of subjectivity, for gender identities constitute the interface of nature as biology and culture as societal roles. Where literary studies are concerned, the women's movement has forced a radical rethinking of the concept of gender, from an unproblematic given of the "real" that literature is held traditionally to mirror to a question of the function of gender representation in reproducing patriarchal relations. The shift in literary studies from the Romantic focus on the author and the creative process to the reader and the process of subjectification is concomitant with the reconceptualization of gender as a critical category. With virtually the whole of his generation, Northrop Frye tended to be gender blind; his work assumes a masculinist and patriarchal normativity in which the feminine is marginal. His writings nevertheless helped to prepare the way for the work of scholars such as Shirley Neuman because they extend the compass of literature beyond received canonical genres. Frye is still concerned with literature in the sense of a particular linguistic practice set apart from all others—with *literaturnost* in Russian Formalist parlance. Neuman is interested in *writing*—écriture—a process/practice through which individuals seek identity as subjects by constituting themselves as utterances in the ongoing dialogue of culture.

Shirley Neuman has devoted the past dozen or so years to a sustained study of life writing, a major area of research in contemporary literary studies. Life writing consists of a set of genres—diaries, personal letters, memoirs, apologies, confessions, autobiographies—through which authors, professional or otherwise, not simply record their life experiences through remembering (or misremembering) and finding appropriate linguistic forms, but seek to become subjects in the world. Autobiography has been Neuman's chief concern. She inaugurated her project with a study of the autobiographical writings of Gertrude Stein (1979) and William Butler Yeats (1982a), both impressive for their scholarship and sensitivity. She has also explored other modes of life writing: in her book on Robert Kroetsch with Robert Martin (1982b), the interview and, in her book on Henry Kreisel (1985) a constellation of genres, public and private—diaries, letters, fiction, interviews, and the opinions of others. Most recently Neuman has edited a special number of *Prose Studies* devoted to autobiography and gender (1991). A book on autobiography and gender is forthcoming.

"'Your Past...Your Future': Autobiography and Mothers' Bodies" deals with gender obliquely in attempts by biographer-autobiographers to confront maternal origins. From a theoretical point of view it raises a fundamental problem: with the mother and mothering, we perhaps reach a limit not only of the literary but of the symbolic as such, the semiosic process of generating identity as meaning. The mother's body, the material matrix of every one of us, is before all tropological activity, all discourse, and all generic realizations. As such, it is unknowable and unrepresentable, an inarticulate substrate to communication, possessed, so to speak, of an infinite and irreducible "Gödelness". Neuman leads us into this labyrinth in which lurks the devouring monster who is also our genetrix. She takes us through a number of biographies of their mothers by autobiographers, men and women, middle and working class, noting the difficulties of trying to write the mother's body into discursive existence in the context of trying to write into existence the self or of trying to honour the mother without violating the self. Biographed mother and autobiographed self emerge as a conjugate pair, each forever threatening to occlude the other.

As points on the path of literary theoretical development and critical practice in Canada since the publication of *Anatomy of Criticism* these essays are exemplary. Frye called for a literary criticism that would be subsumed in a larger project of cultural criticism. Linda Hutcheon's work, concerned as much with the visual arts as the literary and grounded in a general theory of culture, is precisely that. Shirley Neuman's work on life writing genres embodies the corollary to Frye's demand where verbal art itself is concerned—the movement from literature as monuments to individual genius to writing as a process of self-positing in the communal flow of discourse.

* * * * * * * * * * * *

The task, a gratifying one, has fallen to me as incoming chairman of the departmental committee charged with organizing the annual Munro Beattie Lecture to prepare these three papers for publication and provide an introduction. The mounting of the lectures, however, is the result of the efforts of many colleagues. I will mention by name my predecessors in chairing the committee—R. H. MacDonald, who brought Prof. Frye to Carleton (and before him, Profs. Mandel, Fussell, and Bissell), and Enoch Padolsky, who organized the visits of Profs. Hutcheon and Neuman and who conceived of this volume. I wish also to thank my colleagues Gordon Wood and Priscilla Walton for providing essential information, my Research Assistant, Gail Anderson, for the electronic editing of the texts, and Michael Gnarowski and the staff of Carleton University Press for bringing the project to realization. Finally, on behalf of the Department of English, I thank Carleton's Dean of Arts, Dr. Stuart Adam, for generously providing from a very straitened budget the funding that made the publication of this volume possible.

Barry Rutland

Works cited:

Bissell, Claude. (1987). *Ernest Buckler: Rural Intellectual*. Ottawa: Carleton University, Faculty of Arts Lecture Series No.1.

Frye, Northrop. (1957). *Anatomy of Criticism: Four Essays*. Princeton: Princeton University Press.

——.(1947). *Fearful Symmetry: A Study of William Blake*. Princeton: Princeton University Press.

Fussell, Paul. (1988). *Writing in Wartime: The Uses of Innocence*. Ottawa: Carleton University, Faculty of Arts Lecture Series No.2.

Hutcheon, Linda (1984). *Narcissistic Narrative: The Metafictional Paradox*. London & New York: Methuen. (1980) Waterloo: Wilfred Laurier University Press.

——.(1985). *A Theory of Parody: The Teaching of Twentieth Century Art Forms*. London & New York: Methuen.

——.(1988). *A Poetics of Postmodernism: History, Theory, Fiction*. New York & London: Routledge.

——.(1989). *The Politics of Postmodernism*. London & New York: Methuen.

——.(1990). *The Canadian Postmodern: A Study of Contemporary English-Canadian Fiction*. Toronto, New York, Oxford: Oxford University Press.

——.(1991). *Splitting Images: Contemporary Canadian Ironies*. Toronto, New York, Oxford: Oxford University Press.

Lyotard, Jean-François. (1984). *The Post Modern Condition: A Report on Knowledge*. Trans. Geoff Bennington & Brian Massumi. Minneapolis: University of Minnesota Press.

Neuman, Shirley. (1979). *Gertrude Stein: Autobiography and the Problem of Narration*. Victoria: University of Victoria, English Literary Studies.

——.(1982a). *Some One Myth: Yeats' Autobiographical Prose*. Portlaoise: The Dolmen Press.

——.(1982b), with Robert Martin. *Labyrinths of Voices: Conversations with Robert Kroetsch*. Edmonton: NeWest Press.

——.ed. (1985). *Another Country: Writings by and about Henry Kreisel*. Edmonton: NeWest Press.

———., ed. (1991). *Autobiography and the Question of Gender. (Prose Studies* Vol. IX, No. 2). London: Frank Cass.

Thompson, D'A. W. (1917). *On Growth and Form.* Cambridge: Cambridge University Press.

White, Hayden. (1978). "Introduction: Tropology, Discourse, and the Modes of Human Consciousness," *Tropics of Discourse: Essays in Cultural Criticism.* Baltimore & London: Johns Hopkins University Press. 1-25

NORTHROP FRYE

HENRY JAMES

AND

THE COMEDY OF

THE OCCULT

It is a genuine pleasure to be giving a lecture in honour of my old friend, Professor Munro Beattie. Our friendship goes back to undergraduate days at Victoria College, when we were fellow-students of Pelham Edgar. Edgar's main scholarly interest was in Henry James, on whom he wrote a pioneering study published in 1927. *Henry James: Man and Author* is a badly organized book, but it is full of the candour and simplicity which was Edgar's great quality as a critic, and is an especially useful quality for such a subject. Munro Beattie shared this interest of Edgar's at once: I took much longer to be attracted to James, much as I respected and even envied my classmate's understanding of him. Whatever understanding of James I may have acquired since, I have at least read him, so I felt that a lecture devoted to him would be an appropriate personal tribute for this occasion.

It was logical enough, I suppose, for a Canadian critic of Edgar's generation, half British and half American in his own cultural background, to be fascinated by Henry James, with his North Atlantic preoccupations. James ignores Canada, but then, apart from Boston and New York, he largely ignores the United States as well, at least in his fiction. James thought of the European side of the Atlantic as providing tradition and cultural continuity, and of the American side as having a willingness to experiment and opportunity to expand. A complete human existence, then, would be located in some intermediate Atlantis that never quite comes up for air. One can find similar attitudes in Canadian or pre-Canadian writers from Haliburton to Grove and beyond, sometimes with the suggestion that in default of an Atlantis, Canada may have to do instead.

I first became really attracted to James when a student in Oxford, after I picked up, for a shilling apiece, the two novels James had left unfinished at his death, *The Ivory Tower* and *The Sense of the Past*, along with the notes for them that the author had left. *The Ivory Tower*, which I shall return to later, confirmed all the things I felt I disliked about James at that time, but *The Sense of the Past* fascinated me: it was a story of time travel, about a twentieth-century American who walks into the English eighteenth century and exchanges places with an eighteenth-century English namesake equally attracted to the future. By chance a popular version of it, *Berkeley Square*, was running in the movie houses at the time. I could understand James's somewhat possessive interest, in his later years, in H.G. Wells as a writer who could carry on from where he stopped, as Wells seemed to have mastered representational and fantastic themes, including time travel, with equal fluency.

Time travel is one of the major themes developed since by the aspect of science fiction that is really occult fantasy. Another and closely related theme, that of identity in parallel worlds, was also anticipated by James in "The Jolly Corner." These two stories, *The Sense of the Past* particularly, seemed to me central to everything that had preoccupied James from the beginning about the social and psychological culture shocks that the two sides of Atlantic civilization contained for one another. It puzzled me, however, not that *The Sense of the Past* was unfinished, as its theme became almost unmanageably complex even for James as it developed, but that so crucial a story should take the form of what was really a ghost story.

James wrote ghost stories at intervals all through his writing career, and sometimes we tend to ask whether a given story is or is not a ghost story, a question we should never think of asking with, say, Kafka's *Castle* or Beckett's *Molloy*. But the ghost story was a specific English Victorian genre, featured in the Christmas issues of family magazines, and James adhered to its conventions for most of his life: *The Turn of the Screw* is firmly embedded in them. In James's later fiction, in *The Sacred Fount*, *The Beast in the Jungle*, "The Altar of the Dead," we are well past the ghost story, and yet equally far beyond what is called "realism" too. And even in more representational fictions, such as *The Wings of the Dove* or *The Ambassadors*, we become increasingly aware of what Wallace Stevens calls "ghostlier demarcations, keener sounds," as objective and hidden worlds more and more interpenetrate. The reason for this is not that James came to "believe in" this or that, or that he was beginning to prefer one type of subject matter to another. The reason is purely technical: his work was getting more concentrated, and the imaginative possibilities covered increasingly larger areas than the surface story.

James's stories are mostly ironic versions, or inversions, of conventional comic patterns. In a simple comic action, such as a play of Molière, we have, over and over, the story of how a young couple want to get married, but find their way barred by a father with some obsession that makes him want to impose another pattern of life on his offspring. This obsession, called a "humor" by Ben Jonson, acts as a reversing movement, blocking the normal evolution of the action into a state of greater freedom, happiness, sexual fulfilment and common sense, and dragging us backwards into the tyranny of the obsession. The miser in *L'Avare*, the snob in *Le Bourgeois Gentilhomme*, the hypochondriac in *Le Malade Imaginaire*, the pedants in *Les Femmes Savantes*, stand for a tyrannical past, as the normal action represented by the young people struggles towards a future. The "humors" also represent a partial or mutilated existence, in contrast to the wholeness of experience symbolized by the young lovers, who are, in theory, going to live happily ever after once the humor is won over or outwitted. A contrasting comic type is someone, usually a clever servant (*gracioso*), who is sympathetic to the young couple and helps to forward the comic action.

James occasionally approaches the traditional comic form, as in the brilliant *The Europeans*, where old-world people come to Boston, and where there are at the end three marriages, and a near-miss at a fourth, quite in the manner of a Shakespearean romantic comedy. But the ironic variants predominate, and in ironic actions there can be any degree of complication, from total frustration to a split decision. In James the positive goal of the comic action, which in an ironic story is so often missed or thwarted, is not the sexual fulfilment of young lovers, but an intensity of experience that sexual satisfaction only approximates. The vision of this intensity is what Strether, the central character of *The Ambassadors*, sees at the end of the story, and clings to in spite of his growing isolation from the other characters. Again, no scene in Henry James is more powerful than the scene in *The Wings of the Dove*, where Milly, realizing that she has a terminal illness and has only a short time to live, walks through London streets and parks, feeling the atmosphere around her as something so vibrant as to be almost tangible. Characters in Henry James are going through this intensity all the time: the readers can see this, in the long dialogues and explanations in which the tiniest modulations of tone can have a portentous significance. But the characters themselves realize it only very seldom.

The story *What Maisie Knew*, being about a child, is, as the preface explains, the story of what Maisie knew but didn't altogether know she knew. That, incidentally, is the technical reason for an omniscient narrator, to tell us what his characters know but don't know they know, or feel but don't feel that they feel. In several of James's introductions to his works he mentions how the idea for it had originated in the smallest germ or seed of some anecdote, or even a passing reference, picked up perhaps at a dinner conversation. *What Maisie Knew* is one of these "seed" stories, and of his heroine James says after a few pages: "it was to be the fate of this patient little girl to see much more than she at first understood, but also even at first to understand much more than any little girl, however patient, had perhaps ever understood before." Quite a statement when one looks at it. The phrase used about Milly Theale in *The Wings of the Dove*, "the potential heiress of all the ages," fits more quietly into its context, but is startling none the less. In *The Ambassadors* Strether sees young Chad open the door of a theatre box and the author says that his "perception of the young man's identity had been quite one of the sensations that count in life". In short, there is no such thing as a trivial incident: an immense amount of significance is always present potentially, and there are no limits to that amount.

In a story called "The Birthplace" a man gets a job, a tremendous windfall for him, of guide at Stratford to Shakespeare's house. As he goes on, he gradually loses his belief in the historical authenticity of what he's pointing to, and the quality of his sales talk is noticeably affected. A lot of tourist money is involved, so his bosses threaten him with dismissal, whereupon he pulls up his socks and goes into his spiel harder than ever. The implication is partly that the institution is more important than his views about it, his function being that of a guide, not a scholar. But the ramifications go much further. The story never uses the words Stratford or Shakespeare: the locale couldn't be more obvious, but their absence suggests another dimension. References to priests and temples are spattered all over the story, so much so that the reader is bound to ask: what kind of story would this be if this man were the guide to the Church of the Nativity at Bethlehem? Shakespeare is referred to throughout as "He" and "Him" with capitals; there's a comment about how the crowds kill him every day, and so on. So what seems on the surface a trivial story expands into, among other things, a vision showing us how every historical religion in the world has got started, by switching from history to mythology. This quasi-allegorical expansion is not typical of James, but it indicates his direction.

In another story, "The Real Thing," a painter who specializes in illustrations of fashionable life is confronted by a lady and a gentleman down on their luck, who propose to earn some money as his models, on the ground that they have practised being a lady and a gentleman all their lives, and are consequently "the real thing." The experiment is of course a failure, and the painter has to go back to his professional model, the lower-middle-class Miss Churm. For James, as for many writers since, realism and reality are very different principles. Realism aims at the "real thing," the objective world; reality, for a writer, is not objective but verbal. Realism gives us a surface that is "like" reality; reality itself is far more complex. Virginia Woolf's polemic, "Mr. Bennett and Mrs. Brown," is a simplified version of a thesis that James constantly expounds in his prefaces and other critical statements. William James once remarked that his brother's later novels were made out of "impalpable materials, air and the prismatic interferences of light, ingeniously focused by mirrors upon empty space." One may reasonably read two things into this remark. First, William is saying that Henry's characters are treated as though they were ghosts, moving through ghostly incidents and settings in a transparent world. Second, that Henry James is doing with words what, say, Turner in his latest period was doing with paint: not representing objects so much as concentrating on the pictorial elements of colour and lighting.

The characters in James may be good or bad, but whatever they are they never let the verbal texture down. When they engage in dialogue, they "follow" his novel in which he talked to himself about his plans for it. For unfinished novels, such as *The Ivory Tower* and *The Sense of the Past*, such notes are invaluable; for the finished books they were destroyed, but his attitude toward them is curiously ambivalent. In a story called "Death of a Lion," one of the most pungently written of all his stories, a shy, retiring writer is seized on by a socialite who makes him a victim of her parties. In its own eyes her society is utterly benevolent and appreciative, but the effect on him is more or less that of falling into a school of piranhas. He finally completes a manuscript on the verge of death; naturally someone wants to borrow it; naturally he loses it, naturally he makes a half-hearted search for it and can't find it (must have left it on a train). The writer dies after instructing his one real friend to rescue the notes and print them instead.

This suggestion that notes in which the author talks to himself about his book are the equivalent of the finished product connects in my mind with that extraordinary dinosaur, the Collected Edition, where James seems to be trying to transform his entire oeuvre into one colossal logocentric monument to himself. His unwillingness to let his earlier selves die produces a great number of editorial changes that are usually in the direction of altering direct statements to oblique ones. In the prefaces he sometimes expresses regret that he had not eliminated some lively and attractive character, like Henrietta Stackpole in *Portrait of a Lady*, as though he felt some distaste for getting a casual reader interested in his book. In general, the revisions seem to move in the direction of giving the reader the idiom of the author's notes for the novel instead of the novel itself. One disadvantage of James's approach is that the uniform articulateness of his characters tends to make them sound more or less alike when they speak, and the revising tendency not only increases this, but assimilates their speaking style to James's own. I say this because it seems to me connected with the fact that many of his best realized later stories are occult fantasies which could also be read as existing entirely within the central character's mind.

II

In the traditional comic action in Molière and others the "humor", or obsessed blocking character, is outwitted, usually by some unexpected twist in the plot that (as a rule) enables young love to emerge triumphant. In ironic actions the humor is more likely to retain some ascendancy throughout. But in Henry James we cannot have simple humors with simple obsessions, like Molière's miser. For James all obsessions have a miserly aspect, a clutching and clinging to some substitute for genuine human experience. A recurring theme in James is the fetishism that is absorbed by some substitute symbol of the intensity of experience. The obvious example is *The Spoils of Poynton*, where the central character of the story is a collection of furniture, which gets burned up at the end. An early story, "The Last of the Valerii," features an exhumed Classical statue; there is a wax mannequin in a story called "Rose Agathe," a portrait in "The Special Type," and so on. The symbolic objects of the last works, the golden bowl and the ivory tower, have similar connections. So do various morbid fascinations with the dead in the ghost stories, or with, for example, the *Nachlass* of a dead author. Closer to the traditional miser is the role of money in many of the international stories, where, usually, the Americans have it and the Europeans want it. In *The Golden Bowl* Adam Verver, who has made millions in America, retires from business and becomes a great collector for a museum of his own, and his son-in-law, the Italian Prince Amerigo, acquires the status of an expensive but uniquely desirable collector's item. This is only one element in his marriage, but it is the element symbolized by the crack or flaw in the golden bowl that gives the book its title.

Then again, the pedant is a familiar comic humor, but in James many characters who fail to achieve full experience have a pedantic or over-theoretical quality in them, a retreat from a genuine human life into the pseudo-logic of obsession. T.S. Eliot made a celebrated remark about James's having a mind so fine that no idea could violate it. As a character in *The Europeans* says: "I don't entertain ideas; ideas entertain me". This means among other things that the reader of Henry James gets nothing from the story except the whole story: there are no extractable things to be got out of it. James made this point in a spoof or parody story, "The Figure in the Carpet", which turns on a pun on the word "in". A novelist writes a story which is believed to contain some ineffable precious secret—the metaphor of a buried treasure, something to be removed from where it is, is employed. There is no secret, but the belief that there is one inspires a whole cult.

At the same time James's stories are full of characters who are victims of positive gang-rapes of ideas, and will go to any lengths to defend and elaborate them. In *The Bostonians*, for example, Olive Chancellor takes a younger woman under her protection to educate her in advanced feminist views, including the superior virtue of celibacy, with little if any awareness that she is rationalizing a considerably over-heated Lesbian crush. Closer to our present theme is an early story, "Diary of a Man of Fifty," featuring a narrator who had walked out on an Italian countess because she received, and eventually married, the man who had killed her husband in a duel (she said her husband was a brute anyway). Twenty-five years later he goes back to Florence and finds her daughter there with a young Englishman whom he feels to be in exactly the same situation he was. He's so convinced that the situations are identical that he imposes on the reader, who's almost ready to believe that the story is a Kafkaesque nightmare. Gradually it dawns on the reader that the narrator is a nut, and fortunately it dawns on the young man too, who marries the daughter and is very happy with her. "I had a complete theory about her," the narrator says plaintively.

A story called *Lady Barberina*, which is about as near to straight farce as James ever came, tells us of a pompous American doctor who marries a stupid English mooncalf, whose one accomplishment is to sit on a horse while it jumps fences. The American says he wants "race" in his marriage, with the result that his highly unadaptable partner regards him to the end as a "foreigner". This marriage, we learn, is suggested, in fact practically arranged, by an American woman with a theory: she's married very well in England and wants to build a "bridge" between the two countries. In *The Wings of the Dove* Maud Lowder, a socialite, takes the brilliant but impoverished Kate Croy under her protection and refuses to allow her to marry anyone who is not a "great man:" again a typical comic action with a blocking character acting out an obsessive theory. Mrs. Newsome in *The Ambassadors*, who never enters the action except by proxy, has a theory that her son Chad is living an immoral life in Paris, which he is from her point of view, and the whole action of the novel turns on this inflexible and provincial parental "humor". In *Portrait of a Lady* Ralph Touchett bestows a large fortune on the heroine Isabel Archer because of a theory that she will do something interesting with it. She does, too: she immediately constructs a theoretical air-castle of her own that leads her to refuse a most attractive proposal and throw herself away on a broken-down slob ("sterile dilettante," the text calls him).

These theoretical humors have a peculiarly close relation to the occult stories, because the occult by definition is unknown, and what we don't know we are impelled to concoct theories about. In a story called "The Marriages" the central figure, a woman named Adela, is bitterly opposed to her father's remarrying because she's fixated on her dead mother's memory. She admits that her father seems happy, "and it's dreadful of him to want to be." So she breaks up the engagement by calling on the prospective stepmother and telling her a slanderous rigmarole about her father and mother. The stepmother-elect backs out, not because of what's told her, but because she can't stand the prospect of living with such a creature as Adela and Adela's father won't give her up. A relevant detail is that Adela believes that she's in spiritual communication with her mother, but considering what she does the connection seems morally dubious.

In another story, "The Friends of the Friends," which is explicitly a ghost story, a woman breaks off her engagement to her fiancé because she thinks he's more devoted to a dead woman than he is to her. He has seen the dead woman only once, and that was when she came to call on him, apparently after her death. It seems a somewhat strained reason for breaking off an engagement, but the living woman, who is also the narrator, has her theory to safeguard: "Everything in the facts was monstrous, and most of all my lucid perception of them: the only thing allied to nature and truth was my having to act on that perception. . . . When six years later, in solitude and silence, I heard of his death I hailed it as a direct contribution to my theory." One step further takes us to a much more celebrated theoretician, the governess in *The Turn of the Screw*.

The setting of *The Turn of the Screw* is familiar: a governess is hired to supervise two beautiful children, a boy and a girl named Miles and Flora, in a country house. Her employer pays for the set-up but refuses to have anything else to do with it—a convention straight out of folk tale. The house is inhabited by a housekeeper and two dead servants, Peter Quint and Miss Jessel, who have, according to the housekeeper, exerted evil influences on the children. The governess sees the ghosts of the servants at various times, and is convinced that the children, for all their beauty and almost preternatural intelligence, are aware of these influences and continue to respond to them. This becomes obsessive with her, and her reaction to apparent evidence that this is true of Flora is merely an exultant: "thank God! It so justifies me!"

It seems clear that the governess is a mass of sexual neuroses herself, and in general is as batty as a Kentucky cave. One episode will illustrate the point: she sees Miss Jessel looming behind Flora on one occasion: she tries to make the housekeeper see the ghost too; the child is frightened and says "I don't know what you mean. I see nobody. I see nothing. I never *have*. I think you're cruel. I don't like you!" This sounds like what any normal unhaunted child would say in the circumstances: the governess's reaction is to throw herself on the ground and go into hysterical convulsions. At the end of the story she is trying to get Miles to admit that he has been in connection with Peter Quint, whom she sees outside the window. Miles finally answers her question with "Peter Quint—you devil!", where the devil is clearly the governess rather than the evil ghost. The shock of realizing his condition kills him, perhaps: anyway, the story ends with a fully justified governess and a dead child.

If we look at *The Turn of the Screw* from the standpoint of realism, the story can be seen only as the fantasy of a madwoman, bolstered by the gossip of an illiterate housekeeper. One has to think also of the Victorian governess's uncertain hold on the middle class, where servants are always vaguely menacing ghosts, threatening to pull her down to their social level. Much is said about Peter Quint as a "menial", and Flora's outburst is said to be that of "a vulgarly pert little girl in the street." The reading of the story as a straight neurosis was more or less that of Edmund Wilson, who never understood anything in literature except realism, but such a reduction is far too simplistic for James. The governess seems to be telling her own story as a first-person narrator, but her story is actually being read aloud by someone else who knew her, and gives the strongest guarantees of her sanity and responsibility. James himself seems to confirm this in the preface to *The Princess Casamassima*, where he includes her with Maisie and Fleda Vetch of *The Spoils of Poynton*, both impeccable heroines.

No, the governess is rather a Cassandra figure who does see what she thinks she sees, though she may be crazy, as Cassandra was. As Hamlet discovered, it is not always possible to preserve one's mental balance when confronted with ghosts. How far the children are aware of the evil influences around them is another question. Miles may be if Flora isn't: he was, we are told, expelled from his school without explanation, although he keeps teasing to be sent back there. In any case the governess's efforts to save the children are a violation of them as disastrous as anything the dead servants do. She is, in short, taken over by the evil she tries to fight.

Of the many things *The Turn of the Screw* connects with, one is the total deadlock of conventional standards of "good" and "evil". There is a picture by Blake generally called "Good and Evil Angels Struggling for the Possession of a Child." Judging from the various contexts in which this design appears in Blake, the child might be as badly off under the good as under the evil one. Similar deadlocks appear in various stories about writers and artists, though as a rule without ghosts. In *The Author of Beltraffio* the narrator visits a novelist who lives with a wife and small son. The wife has not read her husband's famous novel *Beltraffio*, but she "knows" it's a bad book, and she bends all her energies to keep control of the boy, to the point of sending away a doctor when he is dangerously ill. The boy dies—James is a prolific killer of children—and the mother repents sufficiently to put *Beltraffio* on her reading list. Conventional people's fears of literature or art that they think disturbs their moral values very quickly turn into a hatred of human intellect and imagination, and the conventional person is soon in the grip of an unseen evil force. James's father was interested in Swedenborg, and Swedenborg suggests that we are constantly surrounded by evil spirits, who are there but invisible, like the stars in daytime, but are unaware of us unless we do something to attract their attention. James himself owed something to Swedenborg—Lewis Lambert Strether, the hero of *The Ambassadors*, is named after a Swedenborgian novel by Balzac.

Again, *The Turn of the Screw* is one of James's puzzle stories that admit of more than one reading, none of which we can say with confidence to be the right one. In a story called *The Sacred Fount*, a character at a weekend house party makes up fantasies about other people there, confides them to a woman, and is told they're nonsense. End of long and remarkably pointless story. Practically everybody reads the book on this level—the realistic level—and wonders why James wrote it. But there are various layers of ambiguity underneath. It is true that what the narrator is doing is a parody of an imaginative process rather than an example of it: no novelist goes to work by making up stories about the people around him. But still the narrator's construct has a reality of sorts: it is subjective reality confronted with objective reality, even if the two fail entirely to coincide. Beneath that is a still more elusive question. Why couldn't the narrator's fantasy be a real version of what is going on, told with a different perspective and emphasis? When the woman says impatiently about one of his figures: "there's really nothing in him at all," is she making a factual statement about any conceivable human being? But then we go back to the surface meaning, and realize that is doubtless truth also, if not *the* truth: James has many observers who get things wrong, and was bound to write a parody of the process sooner or later.

Such a story as *The Sacred Fount* brings the relation of reality and realism into sharp confrontation: either there is some hidden reality that the narrator's fantasies point to, however vaguely and inaccurately, or there is no discernible reason for setting them forth at all. This principle, which runs through all of James's work, gives the occult stories a particular significance. A ghostly world challenges us with the existence of a reality beyond realism which still may not be identifiable as real. *The Wings of the Dove*, for example, is not a ghost story, but it is a story of two attractive young lovers, Kate Croy and Morton Densher, who want to marry but are blocked by poverty and impotence. As in a Molière comedy, they outwit the blocking character Maud Lowder, but they do it by descending on a dying American heiress and extracting her money like vultures battening on a corpse. Morton Densher struggles for some sense of self-respect to the very end of the story, but is powerless in the grip of something quite as sinister as any Quint or Jessel. Nor can we identify this sinister force with Kate Croy: she is more resolute and ruthless than he is, but is quite as trapped in what seems to her an inescapable situation. Milly Theale, the heiress, dies in Venice, the city of Ben Jonson's play *Volpone*, where the theme of parasitism is set out brutally with nothing of James's ironic niceties or scruples.

It is also Venice that forms the setting of *The Aspern Papers*. Here Juliana, the ex-mistress of the young Romantic American poet, Jeffrey Aspern, dead for many years, lives with her niece Miss Tina in possession of all Aspern's papers.

An American scholar, the narrator and one of a breed evidently as rapacious in James's day as now, comes to rent rooms in their palazzo. Juliana is a ferocious old harridan who is determined to extract as much American money from the scholar as she can, but has no intention of giving up a scrap of the papers, unless, perhaps, she can benefit her niece, the only human being now that she cares anything about. So Juliana and the narrator settle down to a watching and waiting game. The narrator remarks that the greatest vice is not knowing where to stop, and he is carried along to the point where he is mentally a thief and burglar and seducer of virgins, though he shrinks from the two physical acts of actually seizing the papers and actually marrying Miss Tina. His self-rationalizings get more desperate as the story proceeds. He is warned at the beginning that he may have to make love to Miss Tina: he says he would, recalls this later and calls it a "joke without consequences". He breaks into Juliana's room and is caught by her, but maintains that he wasn't really about to steal the papers, just to "test a theory." Finally Juliana dies and Miss Tina destroys the papers, as she doesn't want anything to do with a man who in effect turned her down when she in effect proposed to him.

The Aspern Papers is not a ghost story, except to the degree that the dead poet may be watching the action sardonically from his portrait, as there are indications that he is. Several of James's stories deal with a dead author's reactions to the disposal of his papers. The fact that Aspern and his ex-mistress are Americans (the originals for the story were Byron and Jane Clairmont), and his period around 1820, brings the theme very close to The Sense of the Past. The story seems in any case as frightening as The Turn of the Screw, and more ambiguous in its moral categories. If Quint and Jessel do exist as ghosts, they are identifiably evil. But in The Aspern Papers there is once again a total deadlock which the categories of good and evil are quite useless to resolve. Modern morality would be solidly against Juliana and for the scholar, because this is an ironic age, which believes that a figure interesting to the public belongs totally to the public, and has no right to the smallest shred of privacy. But at the time of The Aspern Papers, privacy had its rights too: burning one's papers at death was a normal procedure, and for Juliana to keep her lover's letters safe from prying eyes carried its own justification.

I mentioned the Venetian setting of the story, and towards the end the narrator remarks about how "the Venetian figures, moving to and fro against the battered scenery of their little houses of comedy, strike you as members of an endless dramatic troupe." There seems to be a reference to the bedrock of all European comedy, the commedia dell' arte, with its stock characters, its improvised plots, and its close relation to puppet theatre. One is reminded of the ballet-like plots of *What Maisie Knew* and *The Golden Bowl*, with their characters twining and intertwining in symmetrical patterns: a convention that runs all through fiction, especially comic fiction, though perhaps introduced in its modern form by Goethe's *Elective Affinities*, the title of which is a metaphor from chemical reactions. A James novel is "really" a story of forces of demonic evil and angelic innocence sweeping across fully articulate and intelligent beings who are largely unaware of them. It is just as "really" a story of chess pieces moving through an endgame that can result only in checkmate or stalemate. One has to read James by a stereo vision that brings the two realities into focus.

III

Apart from the various "humors", the fetishists and pedants, who fail to achieve any real intensity of experience, is there a general force that acts as a cause, apart from these effects? There are many answers, but one important one is certainly the narcosis of time. We eat and sleep, not when we are hungry or sleepy, but when it is time to eat or sleep, and the habit grows on us of committing experience to time, so that we drift along with its irreversible movement instead of withdrawing from it occasionally to become fully self-aware. The narcosis of time operates with peculiar power in the realm of expectation, where something is to happen in the future, as with the revolutionary programs, feminist in *The Bostonians* and social in *The Princess Casamassima*, that bemuse many of James's characters. There is also a struggle with time peculiar to the writer or artist, where the creator has to learn to relax his will and let things take their own time without drifting into laziness. This theme haunts James from *Roderick Hudson* on: a short story "The Madonna of the Future," is a more conventional tale of an artist (American in Europe, of course) who keeps dreaming of a supreme masterpiece but never lifts a brush. The archetype for the story, referred to in the text, is Balzac's *Chef d'oeuvre inconnu*, but the man in that story at least worked on his delusion. The theme means a good deal to James because he himself was no infant prodigy; he took a long time to develop, and the feeling of having to die before one has really begun to understand one's art comes into many stories, most poignantly "The Middle Years."

But the transfer of experience to expectation is at its clearest in the terrible story *The Beast in the Jungle*, where John Marcher has been obsessed all his life by the notion that some tremendous experience, exhilarating or disastrous, awaits him at some time or other. Meanwhile he passes up every opportunity to achieve genuine experience, such as loving the sensitive and intelligent woman who loves him. Eventually the beast springs, along with Marcher's awareness that its name is Nothingness, and that he is now only a lost soul.

A gentler irony pervades a shorter tale called "The Bench of Desolation," where an elderly couple are sitting together on a bench beside the sea. The woman (I simplify slightly) has sued the man for breach of promise, and he has beggared himself for a lifetime in attempting to repay her—a theme slightly resembling de Maupassant's famous "Necklace" story. The woman tells him that she has carefully saved every penny he has paid her, because she knew more about money than he did, and she is paying it back with fivefold interest. What she forgot about was the passage of time, and that while she was saving his money he was spending his life. No other story in James has quite the eerie, other-worldly atmosphere of this one, in which, as in a Japanese Noh play, we seem to be in a world between death and birth, where all regrets have lost their relevance.

The next step takes us into the "international" theme so central in Henry James, where an American goes to Europe in search of deeper and richer experience. The movement is almost always eastward, and the protagonist is more frequently female than male. Again, the theme is a comic one, and the normal happy ending would be, as remarked earlier, not the right marriage necessarily, but the achievement of some kind of initiation into a fuller life. Ironic versions of this comic theme lead to frustrations of various kinds. One common story-type has the general pattern: naive innocent wealthy American girl goes to Europe, marries some very dubious Count de Spoons character, and wrecks her life.

The earliest major treatment of this theme, I think, is a story belonging to James's Paris period, *Madame de Mauves*. Here a romantic American girl named Euphemia, her convent-educated head turned by historical romance, feels that marriage to a Frenchman of a very old aristocratic family would be marriage to a superman. The Baron she marries is not a superman and his eye soon wanders, and Euphemia's life becomes miserable. The Baron's sister gives her a severe lecture: the male de Mauves have been having it on the side since Merovingian times, and who does Euphemia think she is to object to such hoary whoring? The sister actually seems to think that if a vice has a long enough pedigree it becomes something admirable: an aspect of aristocracy and tradition that the romances had not discussed. An American named Longmore comes to console Euphemia; the Baron has just enough of a conscience to hope that Longmore will take his wife on, but the lady is not for that kind of burning, and talks Longmore into renouncing her. Longmore himself doesn't want renunciation: he wants experience, even if respectable. However, he goes back to America; the Baron then suddenly has a change of heart and falls madly in love with his wife again, but as she will now have nothing more to do with him either he shoots himself. An exasperating story, but significant in many ways.

The generic affinities of the story are interesting. Euphemia is a kind of Courtly Love mistress, covering the entire spectrum of sexual frustration from the ideal of sublimation who demands total renunciation of sex from her lovers, to the frigid ice statue whose cruelty kills or otherwise destroys the essential life of her lover, in this case including her repentant husband as well. A similar figure appears in the Aurora Coyne of *The Sense of the Past*, an American woman who has been to Europe, had some unknown bad experience there, and tries to extract a vow from the hero that he will never go to Europe, though she gives him no guarantees in return.

There are some remarkable episodes in this early story: Longmore has a dream in which he sees Euphemia across water, gets a boat to the other side, and finds she's back on the side he left. Boats and water are often associated with sexual experience in James, whether genuine, frustrated or perverted: they appear prominently in *The Turn of the Screw* and *The Ambassadors*. Another episode features a pair of lovers, the woman socially a cut above the man, who is a fledgling artist, in a restaurant with the woman in charge of the restaurant making dire predictions. In later stories James would not feel the need of inserted episodes to show how the same archetypal situations recur in all ranks of society.

In *Portrait of a Lady*, already glanced at, we have an ironic parody of the type of magazine fiction that used to be addressed to a female reading public, and which usually featured a poor girl who eventually married a rich man, or else passed over the rich man and waited for Mr. Right. Isabel Archer, a rich girl, immediately passes over Mr. Right, Lord Warburton, and a group of American expatriates living in France pass her off on a Mr. All Wrong. In *Daisy Miller* there is no marriage, but Daisy is an attractive young woman who goes to Europe and is ostracized by the society around her for her free and unconventional American ways. She is not really "fast", much less loose: her trouble is that she refuses to think of herself, every moment of the day, as standing in a sexual trap as bait for some eligible young man, and posturing and displaying herself according to the rules of that game. Again the story is cut off by her death, but the essential point has been made. It was made again later by a reviewer who called the story an insult to American womanhood.

A minor and extremely unpleasant version of the same story-type is in a brief tale called "Four Meetings." Here an American woman who has always longed to see Europe finally gets to go there: as the ship docks at Havre a "cousin", a bum pretending to be an artist, descends on her and takes all her money; then she has to go back to America and the bum's whore, who calls herself a countess, settles in on her as a parasite. James says that every unpleasant story should have its beautiful counterpart: I know of no beautiful counterpart to this one, but perhaps the principle he is referring to is different in shape. The positive drive of a traditional comic story is towards a happy ending, which in James's international stories, we said, means an initiation leading to a greater and fuller intensity of experience. The story we read usually tells us of some failure to achieve this, whether a moral failure within an individual character or the result of a sinister or stupid social conspiracy. But we as readers can see something of what might have been achieved, and our wider vision is perhaps the beautiful counterpart James mentions.

Certainly there is a great deal of beauty in the three great novels at the end of James's career, *The Wings of the Dove*, *The Ambassadors*, and *The Golden Bowl*, and there are many suggestions of positive as well as ironic resolutions. In *The Wings of the Dove* Milly Theale, with the hectic flush of death on her, nevertheless achieves a quality of life that carries her serenely over the heads of the lovers trying to get her money. In *The Ambassadors* four major characters all achieve something of the same quality, although their community disintegrates at the end. In *The Golden Bowl* Maggie Verver breaks out of her ironic dilemma by remaining in Europe with her Italian husband and outgrowing her emotional dependence on her father by sending him back to America with her stepmother. Such positive achievements represent an escape from what I have called the narcosis of time, the simple drifting from birth to death. I spoke at the beginning of the ideal fusion of American and European contributions to a full human life as perhaps attainable only in a submerged Atlantis. In Blake Atlantis is the kingdom of the imagination, and the ocean that rests on top of it he calls the "Sea of Time and Space". At some point or other it seems to have occurred to James that the most concentrated possible treatment of his international theme would be one that cuts through our ordinary awareness of space and time.

It has been noted by James critics, Edgar among them, that in the traditional ghost story the dead haunt the living, whereas in James it is frequently the living who haunt the dead. One of the major reasons for well-to-do Americans going to Europe in the first place is to reinforce their sense of the past, to become more aware of their own cultural heritage. So Ralph Pendrell, the American hero of *The Sense of the Past*, having acquired a Regency house in London, becomes obsessed with the pastness of the house, and in particular with a curious portrait of a young man who has turned his back on the painter, evidently as a whim. We gradually learn that the subject of the portrait is another Ralph Pendrell of a century previous, who had come from an earlier

America to marry the daughter of an English family and reconcile the two families. So the twentieth-century American vanishes into the Regency period, while his counterpart moves into the contemporary twentieth-century world.

The former finds himself in a dream world, where everything seems at first to go all right, as so often happens in dreams. Where certain things are not clear to him, he makes mistakes, and the mistakes produce some uneasiness in the people around him, as though they were subliminally aware of being haunted by a ghost from another age. Meanwhile he discovers that in addition to the daughter he is supposed to marry, there is another and considerably more attractive daughter, whom he is clearly going to fall in love with instead. His counterpart in the future, according to James's notes, is considerably displeased at this, and we realize that the arrangement is a rather unfair one: the hero of the story is imprisoned in the past, whereas his counterpart has all the freedom of the future.

However James would have worked the story out, it was a kind of abstract model of the type of story he had been telling all his life. The companion piece, "The Jolly Corner," is an even clearer example of the living haunting the dead, as the hero, an American named Spencer Brydon, who has spent his life in Europe, returns to New York to his ancestral house there, whence he proceeds to dig out a very reluctant ghost of the Spencer Brydon he would have been if he had stayed in America. Both stories leave it open to us to consider their central characters as simple lunatics, but somehow the willing suspension of disbelief does take hold; we accept the exchange of identities in time and space as imaginative realities, and can even see in them a structured form of some of the hidden entities that we get only fitful glimpses of in the more representational stories.

Another unfinished novel was *The Ivory Tower*. Here, for complex reasons we cannot go into, a man named Graham Fielder is left a large sum of money by an American millionaire, has no idea of what to do with it, gives it to a friend to look after for him; the friend promptly embezzles it, and the hero thinks up various reasons for not doing anything about it. He got the money in the first place through the influence of one of the two heroines, Rosanna Spearman, who is a warm-hearted and generous girl, but his affections are clearly moving in the direction of a much more tight-mouthed female who would be more likely to go off with the embezzler. Three books and part of a fourth, out of a projected ten, about someone who seems clearly to be, in post-Jamesian language, a wimp and a nerd. Soon after James started on it the 1914 war broke out, and the book was abandoned. All around him was an outbreak of hysterical fury that made the evil of Peter Quint and Miss Jessel, to say nothing of the evil of people who embezzle money when they are practically asked to do so, look like children in Hallowe'en masks. The well-dressed and articulate puppets were too wooden, too stiff and rattling, for James to have any more interest in manoeuvring them. He turned once again to his ghost story just before he died, because in its fantasy he saw the reality he had sought as an artist, whereas the realism in the social manners of his time had left him with a sense of total illusion.

LINDA HUTCHEON

THE POWER

OF

POSTMODERN

IRONY

It is almost a cliché today to say that irony plays an important role in the definition of the postmodern through its mix of the playful and the provocative. It is almost as if the postmodern existed to confirm Italo Calvino's view that "there is such a thing as a lightness of thoughtfulness, just as we all know that there is a lightness of frivolity" (Calvino 1988: 10). In saying this, of course, I am going against a powerful current in contemporary cultural criticism that argues that postmodernism is trivial and trivializing, and that its ironies are the main causes of this negative evaluation. Marxist critics have been the most stern in their disapproval and suspicion of irony as both a humorous and a critical mode,[1] and thereby they historically recall most closely Hegel's attack on Schlegel's view of irony as irresponsible, anarchic undermining and, above all, not serious (Hegel 1920: 91-2). Yet irony is a dominant mode in much artistic production today, as the twentieth century appears to be planning to go out on the same note upon which it came in. If anything, there has been an exacerbation of the *fin de siècle* thinking: from the modernist remains of Romantic Irony, with its affirmation of (at least) the ironizing subject, to the postmodern suspicion of transcendental certitudes of any kind, including of the subject. Postmodern irony also denies the form of dialectic and refuses resolution of any kind in order to retain the doubleness that is its identity. All this has meant that Marxist critics have likely had little choice but to reject the postmodern. But what such a response neglects—or forgets—is the power of irony as an ideologically deconstructive weapon in the hands of writers such as Bertolt Brecht or E.L. Doctorow or Timothy Findley or Margaret Atwood.

In other words, it can be argued that the kind of objection Hegel had to Romantic Irony is simply not relevant as a response to postmodern irony, which in many ways is the earlier form's very antithesis in political ethos. Romantic Irony has been defined as "an avenue to the infinite, the expression of man's appetite for the boundless; it was expansiveness, it was megalomania" (Wimsatt and Brooks 1964: 380). Postmodern irony is suspicious of any such claim to transcendence, universality and power. To pretend that it is otherwise— implicitly to confuse it with Romantic Irony—not only is historically inaccurate but is also a sign of a lingering nostalgia and even antiquarianism of the first order. While both kinds of irony share a certain self-reflexive distancing, Schlegel's irony wants to preserve contradictions (irony cannot avoid doing so) but aims to transcend them at the same time (Muecke 1969: 159); postmodern irony cannot and does not share such an aim. Modernist irony appears to straddle the two, as this statement from Italian novelist, Cesare Pavese suggests:

> Great modern art is always *ironic*, just as ancient art was *religious* . . . .
> [I]rony discovers . . . a field for intellectual sport, a vibrant atmosphere
> of imaginative and closely reasoned methods of treatment that make the
> things that are represented into symbols of a more significant reality. To
> treat a thing ironically it is not necessary to make a joke of it. (Pavese
> 1961: 161)

There is still a romantic need here to transcend ("a more significant reality"), but
there is also already a recognition of the essential seriousness and intellectual
engagement that were later to coexist with the play of postmodern irony.
Brecht, of course, is the more obvious and important precursor of the postmodern, for it was he who called attention to the political possibilities of
ironic critique that contemporary postmodern fiction, for instance, deploys so
powerfully (see Caute 1972).

The relation between premodernist, modernist and postmodernist irony
has been the foundation of the work of Alan Wilde, particularly in his
important study, *Horizons of Assent: Modernism, Postmodernism, and the Ironic
Imagination* (1981), wherein irony is seen less as a rhetorical trope or structural
strategy than as a historicized vision of life. Premodernist irony, to Wilde, is
largely satirical or "mediate," aiming to recover an ideal norm of coherence and
harmony. Modernist irony, however, is "disjunctive" in the paradox of its
recognition of the fragmented and disconnected nature of the world and yet its
desire to master and control that nature nonetheless through "an equal poise of
opposites" (1981: 10) that results in at least aesthetic closure, if not worldly control. Postmodern irony differs from both: it is "suspensive" in that it is more radical in its awareness of contingency and multiplicity (cf.Glicksberg 1969:
194-5), deliberately refusing the modernist dialectic (which Marxist critics today
attack it for doing). As Wilde implies, postmodern irony is the structural
recognition that discourse today cannot avoid acknowledging its situation in the
world it represents: irony's critique, in other words, will always be at least somewhat complicitous with the dominants it contests but within which it cannot
help existing.

This compromised status that irony structurally cannot avoid, I would
suggest, is part of the reason for the hostility to postmodernism, by both
stern Marxists and by the mass media's current trivializing of irony: for
instance, in March, 1989 *Spy* magazine did a long feature on "The Irony
Epidemic." Both to reject and to reduce are defensive moves, signs perhaps of
a fear of the power of irony—or of its doubleness that refuses facile resolution.
It is not upsetting for the postmodern to have to admit contingency, doubleness,

lack of transcendence—or to acknowledge that "[o]nce others' aesthetic claims are fully ironized, the only thing the artist has left to undercut are his [sic] own claims to authority" (Newman 1985:89)—since it exists precisely to put into question notions such as authority and single meaning. Then, why the aggression? Why the defensiveness? Could it have something to do with a response against what Arthur Kroker calls the "moment of refraction" wherein postmodern irony acts like a mirror to turn the dominant system's logic back on itself—a moment Kroker's own "Sunshine Reports" in *The Postmodern Scene* (1986: 178) illustrate so well? Perhaps.

The negative evaluation of postmodern irony probably has something to do as well with our culture's deeply embedded suspicion of any ironic practice (aesthetic or critical) that might suggest not so much skeptically suspended judgement as an acknowledgement of the validity of both sides of any story— or even of the existence of two sides. This is in no way to deny that irony and self-reflexivity in mass culture (television and advertising, especially) often act as conventions for establishing both complicity and distance, and thus potentially act as "a screen for bad faith" (Lawson 1984: 164) But in what I want to call "postmodern" (rather than simply "contemporary") uses of such self-conscious irony, that complicity is used to create an "insider" position from which to enable a critique from within. Far from being a distancing from commitment and feeling, postmodern irony can be a mode of engagement that uses (in order to abuse) the very possibility of distance, for it knows it is inescapably implicated in that which it contests.

Of course, this means that its power of contesting is limited: postmodernism is not the radical, utopian oppositionality of the modernist avant garde. Instead, it questions the very act—and authority—of taking a position, any position, even an oppositional one that assumes a discursive situation exterior to that which is being opposed. Postmodern irony implies less an "indecision about the meanings or relations of things" (Wilde 1981: 44) than an unwillingness to make decisions about meaning that would imply singularity or fixity. This leads to obvious limits for irony's effectiveness as a political instrument, as we shall see. Irony may deconstruct fixed and single, authoritative meaning, but it appears to have no possibility of agency to go beyond this. I will return to this point later, but it is worth noting here that, for some commentators, this leads to "de-politicizing effects": "that sense of political impotence which the hermeneutics of indeterminacy may serve to valorize" (Bennett 1985: 39). On the other hand, the ironic deconstructing of those ideologies that have proved determinate and negatively determining for certain segments of the population—ideologies such as capitalism, patriarchy, even humanism—is not without political value, as the work of Toni

Morrison, Christa Wolf, or (closer to home) Michael Ondaatje, Frank Davey, and
Susan Swan, among many others, has shown.

What all these postmodern writers share is an awareness of the fact
that, although irony has been linked to mastery, authority, and conservative
retention, there is also a power in irony's doubleness, a power to contest the singleness associated with repressive authority, a singleness that is usually ahistorical
in its claims to eternal and universal value. As Umberto Eco puts it: "the
past, since it cannot really be destroyed, . . . must be revisited: but with
irony, not innocently" (1983: 67). In the ironized (but historicized) work of Eco
and others, that postmodern ironic, doubled discourse functions as "a retrieval
(or repetition) that interrogates the habits of mind inscribed by the past"
(Spanos 1987: 217). Contrary to what dissenting Marxist critics assert, the postmodern is not in the least ahistorical: it merely challenges single, authoritative
visions of what constitutes History. It "does not ignore the wealth of accumu-
lated meaning which grows accretively within a culture. It does not scrape away
in a compulsive [modernist] search for purity but acknowledges and assimilates"
(Shapiro 1980: 8)—but always with irony, as Eco and others insist (White 1987:
xi). Without the irony, the postmodern would indeed be the nostalgic or
even antiquarian beast Marxists want it to be.

Instead, many artists and some commentators have hailed irony as a major
"critical force" (Rosler 1981: 81) with the power of deconstructing that can at
least be the first step to political action, if not a move to the political in itself.
It is a self-reflexive tactic which can be used to point to the fictive status of those
conventions which are usually normalized into "common sense":

> . . . reflexive irony undoes the search for a center [of single meaning] by
> bending that search back around its starting assumptions. The oscilla-
> tion between convention and subject, or between either of these and
> culture, disperses any originary prime mover or first cause and makes
> *the oscillation itself* the crucial constitutive energy of the cultural, narra-
> tive, or individual act. (Siegle 1986: 18)

The oscillation of postmodern irony prevents—to use Michel Pêcheux's (1982:
156-9) terminology—either identification or counter-identification on the
part of the reader, who neither confirms nor rejects the dominant ideology.
Instead, the reader's position becomes a paradoxical and complex one of
"disidentification," working within and against dominant ideologies, contesting any claims to universal and timeless value: "[irony] demands to be viewed,
not as a reaction to a world that is everywhere and always the same, but as the

articulation of man's [sic] situation at a particular time and in a particular place"
(Wilde 1981: 13).

It is in this particularity and specificity that the potential political impact
of irony roots itself. Canada shares with many post-colonial nations a suspicion
of certain generalizing and closed ideologies. And with good reason: historically
these have been associated with colonization and external control over culture.
As some Canadianists have argued, this may mean that Canada is not particularly ripe for what ironologist D.C. Muecke calls "Specific Irony"—a norma-
tive, corrective mode characteristic of "a society with a more or less 'closed
ideology', that is a society whose values are more or less established, whose
members, as a body, are 'assured of certain certainties'" (Muecke 1969: 120).
Nor, however, is Canadian culture particularly fertile ground for what Muecke
calls "General Irony"—the sense of the alienated absurd characteristic of an
"open ideology" which accepts impermanence, lack of transcendence or a
distrust of systems. While Canadian culture shows many postmodern signs of
a deep suspicion of transcendence and authority, its ironies are still mustered
to deconstruct those very things, thus suggesting their continuing ideological
power. As women, gays or lesbians, natives, those of "other" races and eth-
nicities, or simply as Canadians, we often appear to feel the need to deconstruct
as the first step to constructing. It is the deployment of irony, among many other
strategies, that helps give satire its ability to break up, in Northrop Frye's
terms, "the lumber of stereotypes, fossilized beliefs, superstitious terrors,
crank theories, pedantic dogmatisms, oppressive fashions" (Frye 1970: 233).
It is also the deployment of irony in intertextual ways that gives parody the
power Dominick LaCapra describes when he calls it:

> a complex narrative mode involving both implication in the story and
> critical distance from it: a mode of indirect self-reflective discourse
> which, far from becoming fully autonomized or narcissistically specula-
> tive, may be one of the most compelling ways to address (by displac-
> ing)—possibly to work (if not break) through—certain problems....
> (LaCapra 1987: 174)

Irony's double-voicing both allows the distance and makes inevitable the
implication. It therefore allows a questioning from within.

I do not want to suggest that all politically engaged art is necessarily ironic.[2]
The video work of Julien Poulin and Pierre Falardeau is a didactic tool of ideological elucidation,[3] using both art and the artist as active witnesses to society,
yet it isn't necessarily ironic. But as soon as artists today look to examine the

notions of subjectivity, "Truth," or representation, they often seem to be unable to avoid confronting the manipulating and fabricating powers of the mass media, and this is where irony often enters—for how else to deal with something whose impact we cannot avoid (mass culture), while still questioning and even challenging it? The degree of the irony in their responses may vary in both intensity and effectiveness, but it is often not something to be ignored. Michael Snow's use of the *Walking Woman* motif in his work in the sixties provides an early example. Multiply reproduced (in various media), this becomes the ironic repetition of the loss of individuality, of the unmaking of subjectivity, by mass reproductive technology. His *Venus Simultaneous* repeats the figure of the walking woman on various planes of the work, from free standing silhouettes to outlines traced on the background. The reduction that comes with repetition and lack of detail (only the outlines remain) emphasizes what the title can be seen to imply: the archetypal or stereotypical, rather than individual, nature of this woman. Read from a feminist perspective, the irony does tend to rebound back on Snow as a male artist for using such reductive techniques on the female form, no matter how aware he might have been of that irony.

Dave Buchan's 1984 performance "Menswear: A Brief History," offers a more overtly politicized use of irony. Buchan takes on the persona of Lamonte Del Monte (a character from one of his 1978 performance works), the host and narrator of a spoof of that gaudy—not grey—area wherein capitalism meets gender most blatantly: fashion. Here we get ironic inversions of the discourse of men's (and women's) fashion in order to send up the sexist objectification that appears to be intrinsic to patriarchal society. In a related way, though different in tone, Tom Graff's performance pieces turn on ironies of nationality, in particular. His music-theatre works often consist of Graff, surrounded by elegant settings and beautiful people, singing "ironic, humorous stories about Canada, what it was to be in a country so saturated with self-congratulatory but also self-deprecatory mythology" (Mays 1983: 179). Graff, I should add, is an American who moved to Vancouver in 1960—a bit of biography that explains part of the irony here. John Bentley Mays rightly describes Graff's performance work as "art of the borderline. He addressed the question of what it means to be in a place where the border is everywhere in one's life, and where ironic, observing distance from a larger social entity therefore becomes the central and enduring fact in that life" (180). But what happens if that distance is hard to achieve? Does irony disappear, rendered impossible by closeness—or anger or pain? Certainly women artists seem to produce few ironic works about children; writers rarely write about their immigrant parents with irony. One of the ways irony does reappear, however, is in displaced form, or at least with a displaced target. Margaret Atwood takes on injustice to women in a fictional-ized dystopia named Gilead (in *The Handmaid's Tale*); Dionne Brand writes of exploitation and colonization in Grenada (in *Chronicles of the Hostile Sun*). Are they really *not* writing about their experience in Canada, however? There is more than one effective way to achieve even the compromised distance that irony offers.

In Canada as elsewhere in the western world, there are a series of negativized "-isms" that have become the target of postmodern artists' ironies. Among the most obvious to me as a woman is sexism, and the feminist chal-lenges of artists like Joyce Wieland, Joanne Tod, Lisa Steele, Carol Shields, and many others are often articulated in the form of irony. But there are other "-isms", other fights to fight too: classism, racism, imperialism, ethnocentrism, heterocentrism.... Francis Sparshott's poem "Overheard at a Taxpayers' Meeting" (Sparshott 1981: 60-1) reminds us of the creeping power of ageism in our soci-ety. The poem takes the rhetorical form of a monologue by a taxpayer to an alder-man, a tirade against the "senior citizens" in "the old people's home" in the neighbourhood, because "they're getting out all the time." The language used is that which we tend to associate with racist discourse: "something will have to be done about it / it's not nice." The ultimate irony, of course, is that—should we live—we will all grow old, every last one of us. That too may not be "nice" but that irony underlines the short-sighted bigotry of the conformist bourgeois neighbourhood. The barbed ending of the poem changes the discourse again:

> it wasn't to have them scattering all over Metro
> their families paid good money to have them put away
> in Sunset Acres.

The suggested metaphor of the undesirable criminal element that must be "put away" rebounds back with potent irony on the speaker.

There are many other ways in which irony can be used to political, deconstructing ends and there are many causes in which it is enlisted. Gay artist Andy Fabo's work is a good example of how powerful the ironic use of inter-textual references—alias parody—can be. The title alone of his *The Craft of the Contaminated* (1984) recalls Géricault's famous nineteenth-century historical and allegorical painting, *The Raft of the Medusa*. But the representational *Raft* here becomes the self-reflexive *Craft*, and the stress on workmanlike "craft," as opposed to "purist" high art, signals one possible interpretation of the titular "contaminated." Géricault's painting serves yet another function, though. The fact that it has been read allegorically as both a historical reminder and a political statement (about Bourbon nepotism and its disastrous human costs) alerts the viewer of Fabo's parody to seek historico-political allegory as well. And indeed the items on this crafty raft do suggest the possibility of such a reading: a Canadian flag, a teepee, a landscape by Lawren Harris of the Group of Seven. Part of Fabo's "craft" as a Canadian painter, perhaps, is to come to terms not only with European high art (Géricault) but with Canadian cultural representations as well—no matter how historically repressed (that of the native peoples), no matter how clichéd (the flag) or aesthetically burdensome (the Group of Seven's legacy). Does the Canadian content here also "contaminate" European high-art representation?

I introduced Fabo as a gay artist because it is not only nationality that his parody allegorizes. The very title of *The Craft of the Contaminated* suggests something else, for, in our society today, the notion of "contamination" is diffi- cult to disassociate from AIDS. Certainly Fabo's recent work would support such an interpretation. Significantly, however, in order to address society more directly or even more powerfully perhaps, Fabo has moved from painted parodies of European high art to paintings used in video form: his 1989 *Survival of the Delirious*, a video about those who live with and die from AIDS, is a piece that Fabo has made in collaboration with Toronto video artist, Michael Balser. Fabo represents AIDS through the painted metaphor of the Cree demon known as the Windigo. Canadian native art and narrative here replace the art of the European past in a complicated political statement about both Canadian post-colonialism and the shared oppressed positions of natives and gays in our country.

Another gay artist whose sexual identity is central to his work is the pho- tographer known as Evergon. Like Fabo's, Evergon's work addresses the struc- tures and strictures of dominant aesthetic representations of the male and the masculine in ways that recall recent feminist work on the social construction of Woman. An early work, *1 Boy with Ingrown Tattoo* (1971), offers an example of how irony works in this address. It offers multiple parodic echoes of the art- historical tradition of male nudes—but with an ironic twist or two. Here is a youthful, well-built young male posing in a natural setting that recalls classical and baroque portrayals of, for example, St. Sebastian (Hanna 1988: 6). But ironic incongruities at once both inscribe and disrupt this working of aesthetic memory and also encode other signs of a homoerotic sexuality left only implicit in those religious representations. First, there is the tattoo—"ingrown," according to the title. Second, there is the facial expression of the young man: either sensual or sullen, or both. The third incongruous item is the underwear worn by the youth (pulled down around his thighs). Two very dif- ferent iconographic memories come into play here: the conventions of soft-core pornography and—ironically modernized—the modesty-protecting loin-cloths which usually covered male genitals in high-art representations of otherwise naked men. Here his underwear, however, serves no such purpose, as it is lowered to reveal all. Another level of sexual suggestiveness enters with the parodic recalling of Caravaggio's *Flagellation* in the boy's pose. Given the importance of Caravaggio—both in terms of his sexuality and his lushly coloured and textured rendering of male figures—to Evergon's later large-format Polaroid work, this connection is not a gratuitous working of visual memory at all.

The issue of sexual preference, like those of gender, age, and class, has become a topic for ironizing and politicizing in Canadian art in many different media. So too are the issues of post-colonialism, race, and ethnicity. All this does not mean that what we more conventionally refer to as "politics" is never the target of Canadian ironies. F.R. Scott once took on Mackenzie King, in his "W.L.M.K.," as the man whose un-ironic double-talking discourse gave to Canadian history such memorable lines as: "conscription if necessary, but not necessarily conscription." This syntax, as much as the attendant mealy-mouthed waffling, is what motivates Scott's irony:

> Let us raise up a temple
> To the cult of mediocrity,
> Do nothing by halves
> Which can be done by quarters.

It is often easier to be ironic about the politics of the past than it is to tackle those of the present: again, distance helps, be it personal or national.

Saskatchewan Native artist Gerald McMaster's distorted graphite representations of historic figures—Poundmaker, Louis Riel (as in *In His Hands He's Got the Whole World* [1984] or *Riel* [1985])—visually and ironically confront the "distortions" of the official Canadian textbook version of the history of the West.[4] From another point of view, Frank Davey's poems on Louis Riel (Davey 1985) show how the two kinds of distance—the personal and the historical—can work together.

While the verbal obviously has no exclusive claim to the deployment of irony, visual artists often use verbal ironies to make explicit a political point. I am thinking of works like Greg Curnoe's *For Ben Bella* (1965), a painting of Mackenzie King, sitting in an easy chair, but being zapped in the arm by an electric prod held by what is labelled as "Ebert's arm". The image, in conjunction with the titular Algerian revolutionary, is amusingly ironic enough, but the text that

Curnoe paints around the edges is even more so. On the right side, we read: "Canadian $ accepted at par for this object" and on the top and left: "The Liberals sold us to the U.S.A.! The P.C.s destroyed Parliament! The N.D.P. betrayed the C.C.F.! The Nihilist Party of Canada awaits with joy the death of our country and endorses union with our beloved and shy neighbour the U.S.A.!" The internal contradictions here act as the markers of irony for our inversion of the message. In other works, it is often only the title that acts as the signal to be alert for irony. One of John Boyle's *Batoche Series*, done in the early seventies, shows a tiny Sir John A. Macdonald holding up a very large cut-out of a buffalo, on which a run-down wooden farmhouse is painted. It is entitled: *Batoche—from Sea to See*. What the punning play on Macdonald's national dream or "vision" of a united Canada—for which a railway was needed—does is to remind us of the consequences of that "way of seeing". It meant the end of the buffalo—here reduced to a mere outline and surface representation; it meant British settlers and the displacement of the Native and Métis people; it meant, in the end, the events at Batoche and the death of Riel. Macdonald's "vision" is shown to be reductive, lacking depth (two-dimensional), and self-subverting.

The verbal element is obviously not always needed (or used) to signal irony in visual art. Often the materials themselves become the vehicle of ironic juxtapositions. Tony Benner's sculpture *Homage to the White Pine* becomes an ironic "homage" because of how he has chosen to represent the white pine. Normally up to 150 feet in height, the tree here is small in scale: the ironic message may be that we have scaled it down, we have reduced the pine forests by excessive logging. By making his tree sculpture out of metal not wood, Benner introduces another silent irony to protest what human "progress" has done to nature, and more specifically what Canadians have done to their land's heritage of white pine.

Whether the target of what I have been calling these postmodern politicized ironies be national history or policies, gender, race, ethnicity, sexual orientation, age, the environment, or any number of other important issues, what can be argued is that art might be seen as political not only in the sense that it "necessarily reflects the ideology of the society in which it is produced" (Nemiroff 1982: 8) but in the sense that it can be critical of that ideology—in its many manifestations. In postmodern art today, it might be said that the humanist interest in "the moral" has been transcoded into an interest in "the political." This transposition of terms has not been without its obvious problems, however. There is little doubt that irony is often associated with either chaos or revolution, as if to destabilize single meaning were to destabilize social and moral values. But perhaps the fears of the moralists are not without some foundation. As Muecke has argued:

The business of irony is to see clearly and ask questions. Its victims are the blind; its enemies those who do not wish to be pressed for answers. Irony, mobile and disengaged, has always been an object of suspicion in the eyes of established authority and those who feel a need for its blessing. (1969: 246)

If that irony were "mobile" but engaged, how much more suspicious would its enemies be? But does this political use of irony itself not risk falling into other traps, traps such as the complacent smugness and condescending stance of the ironist who feels both politically correct and ideologically self-aware? This is what Wayne Booth once described as the ironist's implied line: "...don't forget that I have a secret wisdom that justifies my ironic stance—I know what is really worth caring about."[5] This is a trap into which readers who "get" these ironies are also not unlikely to fall, at least once in a while.

The other problem or trap is one that continues to bother me. The single most problematic issue surrounding the postmodern use of irony is not its efficacy or its interest as a means of political consciousness-raising or deconstruction; it is whether this "lightness of thoughfulness" can go beyond the destabilizing and dismantling to construct something new. This is the issue raised by Marxist critics and by many feminists as well. If your agenda is action, where can irony fit in, especially if it is seen as a rhetorical weapon of the smug dominant culture, used to keep you in your place? Was Thomas Mann right when he claimed that the choice was between "irony or radicalism" but that we could not have both?[6] Much art being produced in Canada today suggests that irony can play an important role in radicalizing, in challenging ideology, by its power to unmask and de-"naturalize." This may only be a step toward action, but it is not necessarily politically quietistic, as some seem to believe. Art has perhaps never been able to move to agency in the direct way that radical artists and theorists might have desired. This is what Dionne Brand ironically admits in her poem "Anti-poetry" (Brand 1984: 33):

some one at a party
drew me aside to tell me a lie
about my poems,
they said "you write well,
your use of language is remarkable"
Well if that was true, hell
would break loose by now,
colonies and fascist states would fall,

housework would be banned
pregnant women would walk naked in the streets,
men would stay home at night, cowering.
Whoever it was, this trickster,
I wish they'd keep their damn lies
to themselves.

But she will probably keep writing poetry—perhaps ironic poetry—trying always to deconstruct, to undo, to subvert the dominant ideology from within. In a postmodern age, irony seems to have at least the potential to historicize and politicize, and therefore it has at least the potential to liberate what Alan Wilde calls "the blocked energies inscribed in the modernist crisis" (1981: 49).

Endnotes

[1] See Fredric Jameson, "Postmodernism, Or the Cultural Logic of Late Capitalism," *New Left Review* 146 (1984), 53-92; Terry Eagleton, "Capitalism, Modernism and Postmodernism," *New Left Review* 152 (1985), 60-73.

[2] For an analysis of the four bases of political art, at least circa 1982, see Terry Smith, "An Alternative View," *Art Monthly* 57(June 1982): 7.

[3] See *Canada Video: Colin Campbell, Pierre Falardeau/Julien Poulin, General Idea, Tom Sherman, Lisa Steele*, catalogue of 1980 Venice Biennale (Ottawa: National Gallery of Canada, 1980), 33.

[4] My thanks to Allan J. Ryan for this example.

[5] Wayne C. Booth, *A Rhetoric of Irony* (Chicago: University of Chicago Press, 1974), p. 250. Booth is making a specific reference here to the tone of Peter Weiss's plays.

[6] Thomas Mann, *Meditations of a Non-Political Man*, cited in Erich Heller, *The Ironic German: A Study of Thomas Mann* (Cambridge: Cambridge University Press, 1958), 236.

Works Cited

Bennett, David. (1985). "Parody, Postmodernism, and The Politics of Reading," *Critical Quarterly* 27.4.

Booth, Wayne C. (1974). *A Rhetoric of Irony*. Chicago: University of Chicago Press.

Brand, Dionne. (1984). "Anti-poetry," *Chronicles of the Hostile Sun*. Toronto: Williams-Wallace.

Calvino, Italo. (1988). *Six Memos for the Next Millennium*. Cambridge, Mass: Harvard University Press.

Caute, David. (1972). *The Illusion*. New York: Harper and Row.

Davey, Frank. (1985). *The Louis Riel Organ and Piano Company*. Winnipeg: Turnstone Press.

Eagleton, Terry. (1985). "Capitalism, Modernism and Postmodernism," *New Left Review* 152: 60-73.

Eco, Umberto. (1983). "Postmodernism, Irony, the Enjoyable," *Postscript to The Name of the Rose*. Trans. William Weaver. San Diego, New York and London: Harcourt Brace Jovanovich.

Frye, Northrop. (1970). *Anatomy of Criticism*. New York: Atheneum.

Glicksberg, Charles I. (1969). *The Ironic Vision in Modern Literature*. The Hague: Martinus Nijhoff.

Hanna, Martha. (1988). *Evergon 1971 - 1987*. Ottawa: Canadian Museum of Contemporary Photography.

Hegel, G.F.W. (1920). *The Philosophy of Fine Art*. Trans. F.P.B. Osmaston. London: G. Bell and Sons. 91-92.

Jameson, Fredric. (1984). "Postmodernism, Or the Cultural Logic of Late Capitalism," *New Left Review* 146: 53-92.

Kroker, Arthur and David Cook. (1986). *The Postmodern Scene: Excremental Culture and Hyper-Aesthetics*. Montreal: New World Perspectives.

LaCapra, Dominick. (1987). *History, Politics, and the Novel*. Ithaca: Cornell University Press.

Lawson, Thomas. (1984). "Last Exit: Painting," *Art After Modernism: Rethinking Representation*, Ed. Brian Wallis. New York: New Museum of Contemporary Art. 152-65.

Mays, John Bentley. (1983). "The Snakes in the Garden: The Self and the City in Contemporary Canadian Art," *Visions: Contemporary Art in Canada*. Eds. Robert Bringhurst, et. al. Vancouver, Toronto: Douglas & McIntyre.

Muecke, D.C. (1969). *The Compass of Irony*. London: Methuen.

Nemiroff, Diane. (1982). "Maybe its [sic] only Politics: Carole Conde and Karl Beveridge," *Vanguard* 11.8-9.

Newman, Charles. (1985). *The Post-Modern Aura: The Act of Fiction in an Age of Inflation*. Evanston, Ill: Northwestern University Press.

Pavese, Cesare. (1961). *This Business of Living*. Ed. and Trans. A.E. Murch. London: Peter Owen.

Pêcheux, Michel. (1982). *Language, Semantics and Ideology: Stating the Obvious.* Trans. Harbans Nagpol. London: Macmillan.

Rosler, Martha. (1981). *3 Works.* Halifax: Nova Scotia College of Art and Design.

Siegle, Robert. (1986). *The Politics of Reflexivity: Narrative and the Constitutive Poetics of Culture.* Baltimore: Johns Hopkins University Press.

Spanos, William V. (1987). *Repetitions: The Postmodern Occasion in Literature and Culture.* Baton Rouge: Louisiana State University Press.

Shapiro, Babs (1980). "Architectural Reference: The Consequence of the Post-Modern in Contemporary Art and Architecture," *Vanguard* 9.4.

Sparshott, Francis. (1981). "Overheard at a Taxpayers' Meeting," *The Maple Laugh Forever: An Anthology of Comic Canadian Poetry.* Ed. Douglas Barbour and Stephen Scobie. Edmonton: Hurtig. 60-1.

White, Hayden. (1987). *The Content of the Form: Narrative Discourse and Historical Representation.* Baltimore: Johns Hopkins University Press.

Wilde, Alan. (1981). *Horizons of Assent: Modernism, Postmodernism, and the Ironic Imagination.* Baltimore: John Hopkins University Press.

Wimsatt, William K. and Cleanth Brooks. (1964). *Literary Criticism: A Short History.* New York: Knopf.

SHIRLEY NEUMAN

"YOUR PAST . . .

YOUR FUTURE":

AUTOBIOGRAPHY

AND

MOTHERS' BODIES

1: Representation and the invisibility of mothers' bodies

To speak about mothers' bodies in autobiography is to speak from within a double bind in the representational practices of Western cultures. One side of the double bind socially constructs mothers *as* reproductive. Without reproduction, this bind holds, a woman is no mother; without its possibility, she is no woman. Historically, this construction of women in terms of reproduction has been effected by means of religion and education, medical technologies, legal sanctions, and models of psychosexual development which women them-selves have had no decisive part in producing and little control over. In their underlying assumption and in their explicit directives that having a child proves *the* definitive, identity-making event in a woman's life, these discourses see *only* the production of children in the woman who is a mother. But, para-doxically, by emphasizing *what* the maternal body produces—the child—they in fact efface that body and its desires, pleasures, and labour.[1]

The other side of the double bind also works to suppress mothers' bod-ies. Here mothers are socially constructed as self-sacrificing and selfless and, therefore, as without embodied desire or knowledge. Such representations efface the mother's body as the site either of physical responses and desires apart from mothering or of physical responses and desires experienced as part of moth-ering. As Adrienne Rich noted in *Of Woman Born*, there is no room in such rep-resentations for a mother who "feels milk rush into her breasts" or whose body answers her baby's suckling with "waves of sensuality in the womb" (36).

In the twentieth century the suppression in representation of mothers' bodies has been reinscribed and reinforced by anthropological and psycho-analytic theories. These figure the mother in order to justify the son to himself. From Freud to Lévi-Strauss, explanations of the development of kinship structures and the incest taboo as founding acts in the move towards tribal communities and civilization, for example, describe men forging their alliances and their rivalries on the ground of the reproductive bodies of women which are *what* is exchanged to form alliances and *what* is tabooed to prevent male rivalry within the kinship unit.[2] In Freudian and Lacanian psychoanalytic theories, identification with the body of its mother is what the child must first repress in order to establish its own ego boundaries, its first sense of an indi-viduated "self." In this process, the mother remains Other; she never becomes a subject, that is, a woman with an identity and a capacity for autonomous action apart from the child's perception of her as Mother. In Freudian analytic theory, a son faces a second, far more traumatic, repression of his mother's body and her desire. She, Freud holds, fully achieves her psychosexual development and her only "unlimited satisfaction" in life from her possession—at long last!—of a penis in the person of the man-child (597). But *he* must internalize the incest taboo, under threat of castration by the rightful proprietor of his mother's body—his father—and against his own and his mother's desire. She becomes then, in Coppélia Kahn's words, "the idol in which we try to recreate our lost union with mother-as-flesh," in which case the heterosexual male becomes devoted husband-son to his wife-mother, or, alternatively, questing womanizer. Or she "becomes 'the carnal scapegoat' for our fears of the flesh and mortality" (Kahn, 1985: 77), in which case he becomes misogynist and, possibly, avenging womanizer. In either scenario he substitutes other desirable and desiring bodies for that of his mother which remains off-limits in his life and in his representational practices.

This representation, which is of the boy's development and only incidentally of the mother's,[3] subsumes the mother's body to her son's. Lacanian models of psychosexual development up the ante by making access to social discourse—what Lacan calls the Symbolic—the stake gained by the boy's repression of his desire for his mother's body and his identification with his father. This takes the repression one decisive step further by marking the maternal body as that which is *specifically non-representable* within social discourse of any kind because it is what is necessarily repressed as the condition of access to the Symbolic.[4] The analogous hypothesis that the oedipal conflict resolves itself for girls in their identification with their mothers leads to the conclusion that women cannot enter the realm of the Symbolic *as women*: in terms of *gender* identification they have available to them only the presymbolic language of undifferentiated closeness to the mother; in terms of Symbolic discourse they have available to them only that which is coded "masculine."[5]

Feminist analysts have re-theorized this psychoanalytic model in two fundamental ways. They have recognized, first of all, that the pattern of psychosexual development elaborated by Freud and his later revisionists is *not*, as Freud hypothesized, instinctual but *is* a thorough-going and accurate description of the child's development in the nuclear family of the west European bourgeoisie at the end of the nineteenth century (Olivier 1989: 3-5), or, more broadly speaking, of "Western industrial capitalist societies" (Chodorow 1979: 53). Parenting, and childhood development, they argue, are the products of social practices and ideologies and, therefore, are subject to change. Second, they have shifted the emphasis of their inquiry from the oedipal crisis to the preoedipal, or "pre-symbolic" stage, from the nascent ego to the mother's body as originary site of psychosexual development. Luce Irigaray, for example, hypothesizes the "irreparable wound" as not castration but the cutting of the umbilical cord, the act by which the child's body ceases to exist *corps-à-corps* with its mother's (1981: 23). Julia Kristeva posits a semiotic "*process*" (1984: 86), or *chora*, which is "language's underlying foundation" (87) and which precedes entry into the Lacanian Symbolic. Constituted of babble, burblings, nonsense syllables and rhymes, vocal and kinetic rhythms, the semiotic is ordered by the connection with the mother's body (26-27); it is also necessarily renounced by the child establishing his own ego boundaries and identity. In yet another version of "feminist family romances" focussing on the preoedipal stages of development (cf. Hirsch 1989: 130-38), Nancy Chodorow characterizes mother-daughter relations as determined by connectedness rather than castration. She argues that the child's achievement of a "separation, or differentiation" productive of a fully developed subjectivity depends not only on a separation of self from other, but *also* on perception of the "subjectivity and selfhood" of the other (1980: 6-7). Given that, in practice, mothers are almost always primary caregivers, Chodorow's understanding is more "mother-directed" than most (Hirsch 1989: 131), for it is generally the mother whom the child first identifies as "not-me." Where gender identity is concerned, this means that the boy will learn masculinity as being "not-feminine, or not-womanly," "not-mother" and will establish his physical and emotional autonomy from his mother (Chodorow 1980: 13). The girl will learn that to be feminine is to be her mother and will establish more fluid and "permeable ego boundaries" with her mother and a much closer identification with her mother's body than does her brother (Chodorow 1979: 93).[6] This dynamic makes her struggle to establish gender identity easier than her brother's; however it also causes her more difficulty in establishing autonomy from her mother to whom she is apt to remain primarily, but ambivalently, attached.

The scenario of psychosexual development outlined by Chodorow, Margaret Homans concludes, begins "the process of re-presencing the mother's body, over and against the exclusion of it required by the father's law" (Homans 1986: 15), and in the light of our culture's child-rearing practices. It does so by requiring that the child learn to see the other, or mother, "as separate from the self *and* from the self's needs" (Chodorow 1979: 7). But it does not require that the child represent the mother or her needs as *she* might understand them. Both son and daughter, in this scenario, can recognize that the mother is individualized without coming to any specific recognition of what constitutes her particular qualities as individual. And both will associate loss of their own selfhood, loss of autonomy, with reabsorption into their mothers' bodies. As a consequence, the mother's body, however desired as the lost "locale par excellence of fleshly bliss" (Kahn 1985: 77), is also feared as overwhelming.[7] Because the mother embodies the child's fear of loss of identity in a regression to a pre-Symbolic state, her body must continue to be repressed in representation and in order to achieve representation.

In "feminist family romances" such as Chodorow's, giving birth is more than the culmination of a woman's sexual life, however; it is also the beginning of the *social* process of her own "reproduction of mothering." That is, the mother reproduces herself biologically in the child, but she *also* reproduces mothering as a social process. Biological and social mothering link and merge. An intense moment in a woman's gender-identification with her own mother, giving birth also produces gender conflicts which arise from the *social* construction of motherhood: from the asymmetry by which mothers become primary care-givers; from psychological explanations and medical technologies of giving birth and child-rearing; from an emphasis on motherhood as single-mindedly nurturing and a fetishization of the breast as symbol of nurture; and from social dynamics of gendering which make "carnal scapegoats" of mothers' bodies.

All these psychological models, to which our culture has ceded wide explanatory power, rest on the assumption of mothers' bodies as the source not only of life but also of connection for the child who, in the biological and emotional neediness we configure as love, is bound to the mother's presence. They also rest, however, on the effacement of those same mothers' bodies in the child's movement towards self-individuation. Tracing this double bind in autobiography, the genre which narrates stories of self-individuation, we might therefore expect to find mothers, and particularly mother's bodies, everywhere, but everywhere invisible.

2: Sons, daughters, mothers, and the reproduction of mothering in autobiographies: some patterns

Mothers scarcely have walk-on parts in much autobiography, particularly that which stresses the public life of its writer. In the case of businessmen, philanthropists, politicians and professionals this may simply be the effect of a much greater concern to rationalize a public life than to reveal an intimate one. Nonetheless it reproduces the pattern by which suppression of the mother's body is a precondition of public life as of representation.

Michel Leiris is much more explicit about that pattern in his *Manhood* (1984). He does not evoke his mother in his autobiography; instead he tells us that

> I have always suffered disgust for pregnant women, fear of child-birth,
> and frank repugnance toward newborn babies....
>
>   My sister gave birth to a daughter when I was about nine; I was
> literally nauseated by my first glimpse of the child.... Above all I could
> not bear being the youngest no longer.... I realized that I had ceased to
> represent the last generation; it was the revelation of *aging*....(5)

Women, he goes on, remain for him either Medusa, with her petrifying glance, or the *Raft of the Medusa* (an allusion to Géricault's painting of the abject, and cannibalistic, survivors of a shipwreck). Against these two fatal alternatives he erects writing, which he allegorizes as the torrero's encounter with the bull and for which he takes risks which introduce what he calls "the shadow of a bull's horn" into his work and his life (154). Writing and the self are imaged in terms of that most dependably rigid (not to mention murderous) phallic substitute: the bull's horn. Its risk successfully run in a world which, by analogy with the bullring, is exclusively virile; his life, Leiris says, will be gathered "into a single solid block (an object I can touch, as though to insure myself against death ...)" (162)[8] If, as many critics have observed, autobiography is a genre specifically written against the obliteration of death, Leiris makes plain that its primary and, for him, necessary repression is of the mother's body, with its reminder that we are born of flesh and that, flesh, we die.

    When a writer such as Roland Barthes, who has passed much of his life with his mother whom he has made companion, friend, and finally child in her turn, turns to autobiography, we find none of Leiris' misogyny and a considerable effort to attain representation. But despite this, Barthes' mother remains disembodied in his representation of her. In *Camera Lucida*, Barthes mourns his mother by seeking her "essence" in a series of photographs. To do so, he imposes a principle of forgetfulness on "two institutions: the Family, the Mother" (1981: 74):

> In the Mother, there was a radiant, irreducible core: my mother....my
> suffering proceeds from *who she was*; and it is because she was who she
> was that I lived with her. To the Mother-as-Good, she had added that
> grace of being an individual soul....what I have lost is not a Figure (the
> Mother), but a being; and not a being, but a *quality* (a soul): not the
> indispensable, but the irreplacable. (75)

What Barthes has achieved here is precisely that recognition of the selfhood of his mother that the institution of motherhood would deny, but which feminist theorists such as Chodorow maintain is necessary to the child's sense of self. He describes recapturing his mother's selfhood, or "essence" as he calls it, in a photograph of her aged five in a "Winter Garden." While he describes "the figure of a sovereign *innocence*," "the assertion of a gentleness," which that photograph represents for him (69), he withholds from the reader the "Winter Garden" photograph itself. Moreover, he does this in a work that is both autobiographical and a discourse on photography and that reproduces a large number of photographs. These include, for example, a photograph representing the "essence" of a young man whose vulnerability, and whose confrontational and inviting gaze—his eroticism—are embodied in the turn of his head, in the opening of his armpit and slight bend of his elbow in an outflung arm. Where his mother is concerned, however, Barthes refuses the reader any such embodiment. By announcing, then withholding the photograph in which he has found it, he not only keeps his mother's "essence" for himself, but he keeps as the subject of his representation, not her "essence," but his own filial mourning and quest.

However different their motives for refusing representation of their mothers in autobiography, Barthes and Leiris share a self-consciousness about their decision that is unusual in men's autobiographies. More frequently, a son idealizes and displaces his mother's body by means of a veiled identification of her with nature. An aristocratic version of this displacement happens in the passage in *Speak, Memory* with which Vladimir Nabokov ends a chapter about his mother by recollecting her return from an afternoon of mushrooming. The "greenish-brown wool" of her cloak and the moisture on it leave her scarcely distinguishable from the trees seen through the mist "all around her" (1970: 44); the cornucopia of her basket identifies her strongly with a reproductive fecundity the passage images in terms of nature's production of fleshy mushrooms in damp, dark places; her indifference to the culinary fate of the mushrooms solidifies and maintains her identification with nature. The image is tender and idealized; it literally mists over the corporeality of his mother's body by writing a lyricized ideology of "nature" over its sexual, reproductive and experiential capacities.

Daughters' representations of mothers show no more clarity, and even more ambivalence. Resourceful and self-sacrificing mothers whom their daughters nonetheless experience as emotionally and physically dependent abound. The mother may be Gabrielle Roy's, making ends meet in St. Boniface in *Enchantment and Sorrow* (1987) but living out her old age in poverty and loneliness. Or she may be Jill Conway's, shoring up a garden for her family against the wind, drought and loneliness of the Australian outback in *The Road from Coorain* (1989) but ending up addicted and given to irrational and destructive outbursts against her children. In these and many autobiographies like them, the daughter mourns her mother but liberates herself by staging physical escape. Roy's decision, on her return from Europe, to live in Quebec is a decision not to live with her mother but to write, and Conway's move from Australia to Harvard a decision, in part, to "admit defeat; turn tail; run for cover" from a maternal "emotional climate more desolate than any drought I'd ever seen" (232). The decision to escape marks the climax of such autobiographies after which, the narrative implies, the author becomes her own woman, the one writing what we are reading. Often such autobiographies are written by daughters who have preserved their autonomy by maintaining the most complete physical separation: they have not seen their mothers for three, seven, nine or more years.

However great the discretion, tenderness, and respect with which at least some of these daughters represent their mothers, an incipient "matrophobia" is at play here, accompanying and reacting to what Adrienne Rich has characterized as a "deep underlying pull" towards the mother, "a dread that if one relaxes one's guard one will identify with her completely." Such conflicts and fears seem to be lived with particular intensity in autobiography not so much, as Rich suggests, by daughters who "see their mothers as...the one through whom the restrictions and degradations of a female existence were perforce transmitted" (Rich 1976: 235) as by daughters whose mothers have refused some or all aspects of the institution of motherhood. In their autobiographies, their absentee daughters attempt to explain and, often, to construct themselves as, at best, "good" or, at least, justified in relation to women they have experienced as abandoning, or cold, or overwhelmingly powerful.

Among the most negative, and unredemptive, examples of this subgenre is Susan Chitty's *Now to My Mother* (1976), "a very personal memoir" of the novelist Antonia White. Chitty begins by telling us that her mother "was not a good mother to me" (1985: xiii). Cold, given to fits of temper and nervous breakdowns, with practically no contact with her children, Antonia "lived in fear even of us, her children. Later she told me she would stand behind the drawing-room door praying we would not come in" (xiv). Her two daughters project their anger at such rejection onto her exaggeratedly "feminine" body:

> We hated her plump little hands and her small feet in their high-heeled
> shoes. We despised her for not being able to swim or ride a horse or
> even bike. She could hardly walk more than a few streets without
> hailing a taxi. When she approached me to kiss me, something in the
> roof of my mouth fluttered as it does when a cat approaches (51-52).[9]

Just as Susan and her sister project their hatred and fear of their mother onto her body, so Susan's memoir projects her inability to love their mother and her relief at her death onto her corpse in the final words of the memoir: "We moved up on either side of the body to view the face. It was the face of a skull over which was stretched the skin, the teeth just glinting between the lips" (185). In her daughter's exorcism of her by means of the last word of autobiography, this mother has become only matter and *momento mori*.

Not all daughters so relish a mother's death. But where a mother is experienced both as abandoning, because she had obligations that were not focussed on her daughter, and overwhelming, because her own achievements are considerable and she demands their equal from her daughter, that daughter may use autobiography to incorporate her mother's life into her own, to devour, as it were, rather than be devoured. This is the case with Kim Chernin, daughter of Rose Chernin, who organized New York rent strikes in the 1930s and California labour in the 1940s, and who was the first Communist party member the United States government tried, unsuccessfully, to "de-naturalize" during the McCarthy era. *In My Mother's House* (Chernin 1983) begins with a 1974 visit by Kim to her mother, the first in three and one-half years, although one lives in Berkeley and the other in Los Angeles. When Rose proposes that, since Kim is a writer, she should "'take down the story of my life'," Kim responds with all the ambivalence a psychologist such as Chodorow has detected in the mother-daughter bond:

> I am torn by contradiction. I love this woman. She was my first great
> aching love. All my life I have wanted to do whatever she asked of me,
> in spite of our quarreling....
>   But...I'm afraid. I fear, as any daughter would, losing myself back
> into the mother. (12)

The "story" as she eventually writes it is her mother's story, but it is also the story of four generations connected by reproduction but each refusing the reproduction of mothering. In the first section, "Wasn't I Once Also a Daughter," Rose Chernin describes her mother Perle as a passive victim of poverty and an authoritarian, unloving husband and records her own determination not to reproduce that life. In the second section, "The Almond Giver," she describes her life as a Communist reformer. In the third section, "The Survivor," Kim Chernin tells her version of a Communist childhood, and presents her struggle to "no longer [be] the same person" as her mother (282) and her recognition that, no matter how much topographical distance she places between them, she had "brought" her mother with her "in the form of a pervasive and intractable judgement" against herself (288). She also tells of mothering her own daughter, and of the beginnings of her reconciliation with her mother. And, in an epilogue, she records a conversation with her daughter Larissa, now college-bound, in which the daughter's eyes "have a fine, deep glow of love in them" (301). She juxtaposes that conversation with one with her mother, Rose, which concludes the autobiography:

> It is late. My mother is tired. She reaches over to hold my hand.
> Suddenly, she speaks familiar words in a voice I have never heard
> before. It is pure feeling. It says, "I love you more than life, my daugh-
> ter. I love you more than life." (307)

This double affirmation situates Kim as the pivotal person between generations, as the one toward whom all love flows.

The narrative in its entire structure and in much of its explicit content is underpinned by Kim's understanding, first as a daughter, then as a mother, of reproduction as both physical (the production of daughters) and as social (the reproduction of mothering). But this, she insists, is a narrative of reproduction with a difference. Rose Chernin reproduces her mother Perle's encounter with social forces with the difference of resistance—she becomes agent rather than victim. Kim Chernin reproduces her mother Rose's social commitment with a difference—she becomes a teacher, scholar, and poet rather than a labour organizer. She also reproduces Rose's mothering with a difference, delineating a more playful, more harmonious relationship with her daughter than that she experienced with her mother, while also asserting the bonds of generational continuity. She achieves separation from her mother partly through acknowledging her mother's subjectivity, allowing her mother to tell her stories in her own person. But the agency she assumes in the act of writing this autobiography of four generations of women reproducing daughters and mothering also has a side that is less benign for the mother. For Chernin takes control of her mother's stories in at least three ways. First the reproductive structure of the autobiography means that her story has the final word since the fourth daughter has not yet produced either children or stories. Second, Chernin interpolates between her mother's stories her own narrative of their meetings and the progress of the project, an analysis of her mother's character, etc. Third, while she grants her mother her own voice, it is an oral and "immigrant" voice that she transcribes into her narrative. Not only does the question of transcription of an oral voice raise problems about the exercise of authorial power, but her mother's oral discourse is surrounded by and embedded in Kim Chernin's own written and literary discourse. In the shift in the balance of power between the mother and the daughter who fears absorption by her, the daughter's literary account incorporates the mother's narrative of her life.

In the mother-son differentiation and mother-daughter cathexis, mothers have written least of all. Moreover, as Gail Reimer has shown of Mrs. Oliphant, when they have written, neither the genre nor the culture has offered conventions by which to represent their experience of their bodies. Thus Mrs. Oliphant displaces what she calls "the movements...of the body" onto what she calls the "external life" (Reimer 1988: 204) and then follows "each articulation of her own perception of self and world...by a gesture of suppression" (205). Nor has the *reproduction* of mothering been the major theme in mother's autobiographies that it has become in some recent daughters' writing, perhaps because a mother is almost invariably enmeshed in rather than resistant to the reproduction of mothering. Where it does appear, as we have already seen in Kim Chernin and will note again in Joan Gould's *Spirals* (1988), it is inextricably tied to a biological reproduction in which the writer proves the pivotal generation in a continuity of daughters that can often run to future generations.

This is dramatically evident in Rosamond Lehmann's *The Swan in the Evening* (1967), an autobiography of mourning and melancholia for her daughter Sally. Each of its four sections is preceded by a photograph. That before Part One, which recounts Rosamond's childhood, is of herself and her two sisters with her mother. Part Two, which recalls events from Sally's life, is preceded by a photograph of Lehmann with Sally as a child. Part Three mourns Sally as "a young corn goddess" who could look like "an emerging, not yet sun-lit Persephone" (101) and whose life is about to be truncated by polio. Part Four is a letter to Lehmann's granddaughter, Sally's daughter. The narrative of the mother's body reproducing itself from grandmother through mother to daughter and granddaughter, which the previous photographs have established, demands a photograph here of Sally and her daughter, or perhaps of Rosamond Lehmann with her daughter Sally and granddaughter. Instead, this section is preceded by a photograph of Lehmann by herself, about sixty and looking ravaged and brittle through her make-up. Because it doesn't correspond with the section's address to the granddaughter, it emphatically marks the break in the maternal line. Lehmann herself never articulates her loss as a break in biological reproduction; instead she remarks that "Only those born with, and then traumatically deprived of the generative current, the instinct to create in words...can know the strangulating spiritual blockage which such a dislocation can produce. Perhaps purer, more dedicated, less feminine artists...cannot be thus deserted" (89). But the photographs, as well as the metaphor of generation for artistic activity, testify to a "generative current" of maternity as well as of writing which has deserted the "feminine artist."

The writing of such autobiographies and their delineation of family relationships is a largely middle-class activity, even on the part of those who are not themselves middle-class. Regenia Gagnier (1989) notes that a significant portion of working-class autobiographers adopt writing as a tool to help them restructure their lives in accord "with middle-class ideology..., especially with respect to the development of parent/child relations and material progress" (47). The reproduction of mothering which I have been documenting here, as well as the virtual invisibility of mothers' bodies, is a representation of motherhood socially constructed as a middle-class ideal that takes middle-class aspirations, education, privacy and income to live up to. That ideal is not only demanding but is also powerfully distorting of the actual experiences of many mothers and children. I want now, briefly, to turn to several autobiographies which are anomalous in terms of these general patterns I have been outlining and which raise questions about mothers' bodies as they are socially constructed and as they are experienced, in however repressed a manner, in three different situations: those where the mother is working-class, those where the mother is murderously unmotherly, and those where mothers attempt to write their actual physical and emotional experiences of mothering against the grain of our culture's discourse of motherhood.

3: Middle-class autobiographers represent their working-class mothers

Born in 1900, Edward Dahlberg was the illegitimate son of the Jewish proprietess of the Star Lady Barbershop in Kansas City. Like Michel Leiris, he knows that to be flesh is to die: "The real truth," he tells us in *Because I Was Flesh*, "is that my priapic, Socratic syllogism has always been: I have secret parts, I am ashamed of them, therefore I am mortal" (1959: 130). Like Leiris, he writes autobiography to mitigate and transform mortality. But he differs from Leiris in his rewriting of the Socratic directive to "Know thyself"; in Dahlberg's version, "All wisdom is sensual since it comes from the body" (44). Or, to be precise, from his mother's body: "whatever I imagine I know is taken from my mother's body, and this is the memoir of her body" (4).

"My mother," he introduces her, "had two miserable afflictions, neither of which was she ever to overcome: her flesh—which is my own—and the world, that cursed both of us" (3). In this "memoir of her body," he sets himself the task of bringing flesh and world into relation through language. But he also aims to rehabilitate Lizzie Dahlberg as a 'good mother' so that, at forty, he can acknowledge that his face was "dominated" by the features of his mother for whom he was "searching" (227).

The fear that his mother "will disappear" (226) haunts his memoir, and indeed, in her old age she does disappear to him for, unable to "handle her pain" (226), he ceases to see her even when she is present. A dream clarifies this "disappearance" as the child's loss of the nurturing breast:

> One night...I dreamt I saw a woman who was only two empty udders; I
> imagined I beheld her, but there was no mouth or chin or cheeks in
> her. As I grieved for her, water grew around me....I endeavored to walk
> in the water toward her to give her a filial kiss to restore the mouth, the
> cheeks and chin that were—but the waves held me back so that I could
> not reach her. Then I saw a cruse of water and a loaf of bread, and I
> awoke and moaned, "She is dead, and the bottle of water and the bread
> she has left me are for my hunger." (227-8)[10]

Getting up, he searches for his mother whom he meets on the street, "carrying two milk bottles under her arm." His response on finding her suggests that it is her approaching death, and its final withdrawal of nurturing, that Edward cannot forgive. "'What are you doing with those two empty udders?'" he asks her. "Startled when I heard these words, I grasped the bottles from her and ran back to the flat....I tried to shape the face I could not collect. I had resolved to kiss her hands when I saw her, but...I could not forgive her—but for what I did not know" (228). Only after she dies, when he has come to terms with the fact that she lives on in his body, can he both separate from her and connect with her.

A scene of assumption, worthy of the Virgin Mother herself, closes this autobiography:

> When the image of her comes up on a sudden—just as my bad demons
> do—and I see again her dyed henna hair, the eyes dwarfed by the
> electric lights in the Star Lady Barbershop and the dear, broken wing of
> her mouth, and when I regard her wild tatters, I know that not even
> Solomon in his lilied raiment was so glorious as my mother in her rags.
> *Selah.* (233-34)

This benediction for his posthumously idealized mother, however, concludes a memoir which has been strongly marked by Dahlberg's humiliation by her class, age, and race-insribed body. Positively, she is that nurturing "Mary who poured the ointment on the head of Christ" (18), as she annoints the head and necks of her barbershop clients. And Dahlberg rejoices with her that "health was her beauty" (3) and that she took "pride in her vigor" (46). But when the signs of race, age and economic hardship mark her flesh, his reaction is more ambivalent:

> My mother's long nose sorely vexed me. I don't believe I ever forgave
> her for that, and when her hair grew perilously thin, showing the
> vulgar henna dye, I thought I was the unluckiest son in the
> world....Aside from her unchristian nose, what troubled me enor-
> mously was her untidiness. She...dressed like a rag-raker or a chimney
> sweep. I was ashamed when we walked together in the streets.... (3)

He does come to understand "that his mother was arrayed in broken and for-lorn rags because her life was in tatters" (205); nonetheless, he never stops rail-ing at her shamble of loneliness," her "begrimed and nibbled coat" (232), her "sick, sniveling stockings," the "pile of dishes filled with the leftover carrion of several meals" (205), or her copy of *Tristram Shandy* in the oven along with dried orange peels and toastcrumbs. When he represents his life with her with an eso-teric learnedness that invokes an hermetic, exclusively masculine and misog-ynist literary tradition, Dahlberg not only separates from his mother's body in order to construct himself as masculine;[11] he also flees from the race, class and inevitable death the flesh of his mother—"that *mater dolorosa* of rags and grief" (4)—embodies.

That revulsion and flight, however, are complicated by the fact that Edward owes his very birth to his mother's being "a lady-barber Magdalene" (17). Hers is a "carnal" body (43), the lust of which she constantly seeks to sat-isfy more or less respectably in a world where women can still sue for breach of promise and "heart damage" because it is understood that they exchange their bodies for the assured income of marriage.[12] She ruptures the institution of motherhood with its repression of women's bodies and propels herself out of the middle class by *acting* on her desires, abandoning her two sons and a husband who "could provide her with food but not with fuel" (7) in order to run off with a man who would soon abandon her in her turn. Edward is the son of her car-nal break with the institutions of marriage and motherhood and his birth the visible sign of her consequent *déclassement*. Later she will place him in an orphanage for six years because she has taken up with a river-boat captain who doesn't want her child. Over and over again during his childhood, behaviour socially defined as "unmotherly" forces Edward to recognize his mother's body as a sexual body and a working body and, therefore, as connected with his own. If that recognition provokes his revulsion, it also gives him his "knowledge" that he *is* flesh and, as the verse from Psalms which he cites as his first epigraph has it, "a breath that passeth away and cometh not again."

For daughters, too, the body of the working-class mother, whom economic demands and personal desires push to "unmotherly" behaviour and attitudes, can become an object of active revulsion. In *Landscape for a Good Woman*, for example, Carolyn Steedman describes her own "refusal" of her mother's body. Far more clearly than Dahlberg, she understands that refusal as a

> recognition of the [economic] problem that my own physical presence represented to her; and at the same time it was a refusal of the inex- orable nature of that difficulty, that it would *go on* like that, that I would become her, and come to reproduce the circumstances of our straitened, unsatisfying life (1986: 94-95).

Steedman reads her mother's body as economically constructed in terms of the exchange value of a triple labour: the labour of birth, domestic labour, and marketplace labour. In each of these, the working-class woman's reproductive body is what she owns, the goods with which she can make herself "both the subject and object of her own exchange" (82).

One strategy of exchange, one way of "working on the body" for women, has been dress. "Women," Steedman generalizes rather optimistically, "are...without class, because the cut and fall of a skirt and good leather shoes can take you across the river and to the other side: the fairy-tales tell you that goose-girls may marry kings" (15-16). First, however, one must procure the well cut skirt and good leather shoes. That demand constructs Steedman's mother, and to some extent Steedman herself, in terms of consumer longing. Her mother longs specifically for a New Look skirt, emblem of a conspicuous consumption unavailable to the economic resources of the working-class woman.[13] The specificity of that longing shaped her own childhood, Steedman tells us (6), for she and her sister were "the two living barriers to twenty yards of cloth" (30).

If the daughter's body, needing to be fed and sheltered, represents the insuperable barrier to the fashionable skirt, it nonetheless enables a different exchange available to reproductive women. Her mother intends Carolyn as the "exchange" that will force her father into marriage. When "the ploy" (39) fails, Carolyn becomes "both desired and a burden" (17), with desire and burden both figured in the precise economic terms of child support: "We were an insurance, a roof over her head, a minimum income" (57). This recognition produces Steedman's sense of her own body as what is owned by her mother and also leads her to identify her body with her mother's: "she made me believe that I was her: her tiredness, the pain of having me, the bleeding, the terrible headaches. She made me good because I was a spell, a piece of possible good fortune, a part of herself that she exchanged for her future: a gamble" (141). This sense of herself as both her mother's body and as a product with exchange value is part of what Steedman refuses when she refuses herself to mother.

She constructs her refusal, as she constructs her mother's reproductive body, in both emotional and economic terms, noting that "Under conditions of material poverty, the cost of most childhoods has been most precisely reckoned, and only life has been given freely" (108). That reckoning qualifies her under-standing of the maternal body as nurturing; her mother's breasts

> symbolize her ambivalence towards my existence. What came free
> could be given freely, like her milk: loving a baby costs very little. But
> feeding us during our later childhood was a tense struggle between
> giving and denial....I knew this, I think, when I conjured her under the
> kitchen table, the thin wounds across her breasts pouring forth blood,
> not milk. (93)

In this vision, Carolyn recognizes in her mother a woman "who had children, but who also, in a quite particular way, didn't want them" (6).[14] And, in her mother's reiterated injunction, "Never have children, dear; they ruin your life!", she understands both an economic self-construction *and* a rupture of the generational link on which the reproduction of mothering depends, each of these effects initiated as much by her mother as by herself. In this world in which social class constrains the maternal body and its children, "the story of Demeter and Persephone cannot be made to serve a mythic function because it is not a true story: it is not about what has happened, or what is bound to happen. It does not...take into account refusal" (88).

Dahlberg reconstructs the subjectivity of his mother's sexual and work-ing body, Steedman of her mother's labouring body as object of self-exchange; both introduce a gap of "not-mothering" between the bodies of mother and child. But their relation to their understanding of their mothers' bodies is quite different. Dahlberg's is a memorial work, impelled by his desire to rep-resence his mother and to exorcise through confession his remorse for filial ambivalence. It remains an intensely personal work, at least in part because, sep-arated from his mother by, among other things, his identification with the highly "masculine" discourse of prophecy, scriptural allusion and hortatory rhetoric in which he is re-presenting her body, her "quality," he does not address the *institution* of motherhood. For the woman autobiographer such as Steedman, however, autonomy and identification are not such clear-cut issues. Personally, she has separated herself from her mother by entering the professional class, by staying away for years at a time, *and* by refusing to herself become a mother. Such decisions are the kind *not* represented or perhaps representable in the social discourse within which mothers and mothers' bodies are constructed. She makes her personal experience intelligible, therefore, by placing it in the context of a scholarly analysis of the *specificity* of that experience as compared to institutionalized representations of social class, mothering and the reproduction of mothering: she writes a work of sociology for which her own autobiography is the data. Dismantling by means of scholarly analysis the ways hers and her mother's working-class experience call those representations into question, she acts against them to exert control over her own life by refusing her culture's social construction of motherhood.

4: Murderous mothers

Edward Dahlberg dreams of a faceless mother with empty udders. Carolyn Steedman visualizes her mother's breasts pouring forth blood. Clearly, however much these children resist reabsorption into their mothers' bodies and lives, they also fear that their mothers may withhold the nurture of their bodies. They fear that their mothers will neglect or even kill what they have borne. In *Home to the Wilderness*, for example, Sally Carrighar recounts how not she, but her mother, sought to put distance between them.

> If I walked to her she would move away with a rejecting throw of her
> hand....sometimes I wished so much to be near her that I would come
> up to her knee. With a shudder, as if she had been touched by a snake
> or lizard, she would start up from her chair.... She would not make my
> dresses...because she would have to touch me in fitting them. This
> repugnance became even stronger as she grew older. When she was
> ninety...I thoughtlessly put my hand under her elbow as she was
> stepping down from a curb. With a spasm of loathing she went rigid
> from head to foot.... (1973: 8)

At another juncture, after Mrs. Carrighar fails to come to her aid when she is caught in a cyclone, Sally realizes that her mother wishes she were dead. And indeed, at moments her mother's desire for her death becomes "uncontrollable" (8): Mrs. Carrighar feeds her smaller and smaller portions until she becomes anaemic and bedridden; she beats her daughter viciously; once she strangles her, stopping only when someone walks into the room. She tellingly observes that *It is likely that many people who seem to die natural deaths have in fact been poisoned by their families,* a phrase which ruptures the narrative of *Home to the Wilderness* over and over again to signal Sally's recognition that her life is always in danger from her mother.

Carrighar, citing chapter and verse from medical literature, attributes her mother's murderousness directly to the "terrifying, traumatic experience" of her own "dreadful birth," the pain of which her mother frequently recalls, and during which the doctor broke her coccyx by the use of high forceps (9). She finds further cause for it in the fact that the difficult birth produced not the beautiful child she had expected but one whose face had been flattened and whose nervous system, briefly deprived of oxygen, had been rendered oversensitive to stimulation. But despite her understanding—or rationalization—that her mother's "aversion was almost entirely a physical, neurological thing" (243), and not unexpectedly, Sally refuses to reproduce mothering. The deliberation behind this decision she makes plain by an incident in a San Francisco streetcar in which she watches a mother and daughter:

> The daughter was haranguing the mother with so much venom that I wondered what her attacks would be like when the two were alone....
>
> I felt...that I was seeing what my own life could become if I ever should have a daughter. Family traits sometimes skip a generation and my mother's granddaughter could inherit her temperament. Then...my life could end as it had begun (178-79).

Resolving "never [to] risk being trapped in a family again" (79), she finds a "home," and by metaphoric implication, a "mother" in the natural world to which she retreats, and which, even in the most dangerous circumstances, is governed by codes she finds more predictable and just than were those of her home.

Like Carrighar, Marie Cardinal experiences her mother's "very rich and tempting body" (1983: 105) as out of bounds.[15] Again like Carrighar, she diagnoses a gap between the woman her mother "had wanted to bring into the world" and herself (66-67), a gap which meant that her love for her mother "was not, apparently, the right key" (70). Unlike Carrighar, Cardinal does reproduce, but against herself and in her own body rather than against her children, the murderous mothering she has received. *The Words to Say It (Les Mots pour le dire)* opens with thirty-year old Marie "on a couch, curled up, like a fetus in a womb"

(12), speaking to the psychiatrist she will visit three times a week for the next seven years. She tells a story of blood. She has been bleeding almost constantly since the birth of her third child when she was twenty-seven: "I had stained so many easy chairs, straight-back chairs, sofas, couches, carpets, beds! I had left behind me so many puddles, spots, spotlets, splashes and droplets, in so many living rooms, dining rooms, anterooms, halls, swimming pools, buses, and other places. I could no longer go out" (4). A gynecologist has told her "'The only thing the matter with you for now is a fibroid uterus. But I advise you to get rid of it right away'" (7). Her psychiatrist tells her, "Those are psychosomatic disorders. That doesn't interest me. Speak about something else" (32). The bleeding stops; for the next seven years they address "the constant anxiety, the perpetual fear, the self-disgust which finally blossomed into madness" (140) and which Marie has named the Thing.

Behind this presenting symptom of Marie's reproductive body stands a narrative related by Marie's mother about her own body. At twenty, this mother has already lost one daughter to tuberculosis, contracted from the child's father who had not confessed to being ill. At twenty-three she has a son. At twenty-seven, in the midst of divorcing her husband, out "of their wretched desire and their enmity" (53), she conceives Marie. When Marie reaches puberty, as part of her education about the threats sexuality poses to women's lives, her mother tells her the story of her gestation. She tells it, her gloved hands resting on a balustrade, in the middle of a raucous Algerian street. Holding that abortion is a sin, she explains that "It is possible, however, to lose the baby naturally," in which case "it's no longer a sin, it's nothing, it's an accident, that's all" (135). She goes into detail about her attempts to "lose" Marie:

> "I went to find my bicycle, which had been rusting away in the shed for I don't know how long, and I pedaled off into the fields, into the land being cultivated, everywhere. Nothing. I rode horseback for hours: jumping, trotting. Nothing happened, believe me. Nothing....I went to play tennis in the hottest part of the day. Nothing. I swallowed quinine and aspirin by the bottle. Nothing....
>
> "After more than six months of treatment, I had to resign myself to the obvious" (136).

Marie perceives the "beastliness" of this account not in her mother's desire to abort her, but in her first "not having followed through on her desire.... Then, in having continued to project her hatred onto me when I was inside her, and, finally, in having chosen to speak of her wretched crime, her weak attempts to murder me" (140). She experiences that speaking as a dis-membering that, in this autobiography, looks forward to the atrocities of the Algerian war and her own expulsion from the country she identifies as her "real mother" (88):[16] "There on the street, in a few sentences, she put out my eyes, pierced my eardrums, scalped me, cut off my hands, shattered my kneecaps, tor-tured my stomach, and mutilated my genitals" (135). Only when, venturing at nineteen on love-making, she has her first anxiety attack, will she experience that same mother as compassionate and composed, although also as "sadly ten-der and lamentably smug," offering a "complicity...of love and attention" (41) that Marie has never been able to win by being good: by "this intimacy which she offered me that night, I understood that she had conferred death upon me at my birth, that what she wanted me to give back to her was death, that the bond between us, a bond I had tried so hard to discover, was death" (42).

These events which initiate Marie's psychosis find a counter-impetus in two views of her mother which come when Marie is near the end of her analysis. In the first of these, she opens her front door to see her mother who has been staying with her for several days,

> facing me, sitting on her bed as usual. Her nightgown had been pulled
> up over her stomach, so that I could see her hairless vagina. She had
> done it where she sat, and her shit was oozing out down to the floor.
> On the table, beside her, there were two square bottles of rum, one
> empty, the other half-full.... (281)

Recognizing that her mother is in the grip of the Thing, and that it is this that she has passed to her daughter, Marie refuses to take up this reproduction of mothering with the violence and madness it engenders. Instead, she tries to bring her mother "back to the surface" with a phrase one does not use to one's mother—"My poor mother, you are as drunk as a horse's ass" (282)—and arranges for her care elsewhere.

In the second view of her mother, the latter describes her life to the last doctor she visits. She speaks of nursing the ill in the Algerian casbahs, of her hus-band, of her dead daughter, of her childhood, of her son after whose birth "her life had stopped" (288), but never of the daughter who had been such a tenacious fetus and who still sits with her. "Until that instant," Marie writes, "she had been my mother and only my mother, not a person.... In this Parisian doctor's office, I met for the first time Solange de Talbiac (a name straight out of an operetta!) called 'Soso' by her friends" (287). Marie's recognition of the subjectivity of this person apart from her own relation to her as mother, and her mother's death shortly after, allow her to speak her love for the several people her mother was, to tame the Thing, and to leave the psychiatrist's office "born."[17]

Abortion, hysterically figured on the body, now becomes a figure for liberation in Cardinal's metaphor for that phase of psychoanalysis in which the patient relives with the analyst former traumatic events in order to free herself of their phobic effects: "I had aborted myself" (165), she claims. Writing autobiography, Marie Cardinal writes a narrative of rebirth against her mother's narrative of misbirth. But, at the same time she mourns her mother, a process another recent autobiographer, Joan Gould, insists must take place irrespective of whether parent and child love or even like one another. "When I say mourn," Gould specifies of her own mother, Marion,

> I don't mean that I'd miss this woman and the aggravation we caused each other. I mean we need to see the parent whole at last, free of the emotional pratfalls of liking and not-liking. In short, the child must remember the parent—which means put back together the parts, or members, that have only been seen separately until that point (1988: 34).

In *Spirals* Gould mourns and re-members Marion, a mother who never admired her, who never accepted a gift from her with pleasure, who threw into the garbage everything her daughter wrote, who gave her last commendation— "what a good girl you've been"—to a hired companion whom "she didn't even like" rather than to the daughter who had waited years for such words (298). But when Gould begins to see her mother's subjectivity as independent of her own, she understands her as a twenty-year old girl, "her menstruation corked up while she was still on her honeymoon" (206), a girl afraid she would lose her new husband, a girl for whom her "untimely" (206) daughter's birth is, in fact, a kind of death, as the analogous scene in which she dies on her commode implies. "Like childbirth," her daughter Joan thinks, "while the doctor's voice calls out in triumph 'Here it comes!'... what the woman on the table feels, with her knees pulled up, is an urge to unblock her bowel of the biggest movement of her life, a movement that will never come out, that's how big it is" (295-96).[18] Remembering her dead mother, she acknowledges that Marion "wasn't a mother now and probably never had been—in fact, couldn't have been a mother, no matter what she intended—since she was only a child herself" (277). And, waiting in the hospital for her own daughter to give birth to another daughter, Gould recalls the middle-class institution of motherhood of her mother's time, in which a new mother received hospital visitors while her baby lay in the nursery, then went home to a cook and a nurse, each much more experienced than she and much more able to care for her newborn. She realizes that these social arrangements prevented her mother from learning to nurture and from developing what Kristeva calls the semiotic language of mother-infant bonding and what Gould describes as "a slippery babble full of vowels: private babble on her part, mews or cries on mine, some mouth work we missed" (216). Few passages in autobiography present so concisely the ways in which the social practices of motherhood can close off the very connections they are meant to sanctify by repressing physical cognition of birthgiving and nurturing.

5: Mothers thinking through their bodies

In the reproduction of mothering, daughters such as Marie Cardinal and Joan Gould are also mothers who must re-think, and think through, their practices of mothering and their mothering bodies if they are not to reproduce the mothering that has caused them pain as daughters. Joan Gould writes as a woman making the transition from mother to grandmother. In the four generations that extend from her mother to her granddaughter, her mothering is over. At the moment her daughter gives birth, she has "finished giving birth to [her] daughter" (221); now hers is the part of watching her granddaughter play between her daughter's legs as the two share a bath. Gould's sense of her body as chiefly reproductive body is strong and unquestioned in *Spirals*; the crux of her narrative is the problem of how she can *be* a mother at a time when the balance of power has shifted from her to her children, when they maintain their autonomy, and when they have taken over the reproduction of mothering. Her task is to do what her children have already done, to give up the "passionate, horizontal and immediate, flesh to flesh" (215) bonding of mother and child, and to establish her own autonomy from motherhood by giving "birth" to herself as her "own last child" (234).

For Marie Cardinal, thinking through her own mothering body involves recognizing and politicizing the long labour that she began *after* she left the delivery room and that the social construction of motherhood does not even recognize *as* labour. She understands that "outside in the streets and in the stores, at the office and in the house,"

> what it meant to be a woman was to have a vagina. Until then I had
> never questioned the notion of femininity, that specific quality of being
> human having to do with breasts, long hair [etc]....Dressed, scented,

embellished like a shrine, fragile, precious, delicate, illogical, bird-brained, available, the hole is always open, always ready to receive and to give.

It wasn't true! I knew what it was to be a woman. I was one of them. I knew what it meant to wake up in the morning before the others, to get breakfast, to listen to the children, who all want to talk at the same time. Ironing at daybreak, mending in the early morning, homework at dawn (1983: 261-62).

And so on, through laundry, cleaning, grocery shopping, preparing lunch, doing "the only work that counts, the work you're paid for, without which there would be black misery," doing errands, listening to children, preparing dinner, supervising more homework, bathing children, and

giving out kisses when all you want is to sleep, to rest. Have a guilty conscience because of it, play the game, regret not getting anything out of it, fear another pregnancy....

That's what it means to have a vagina. (263)

This countering of idealization with physical experience leads to a dream which re-writes Freud and provides for her own agency in constructing the motherhood within which she will live. She dreams of a snake rising between her thighs, which she and her husband destroy when he puts his fingers beside hers on its neck and pulls "until the snake divides in two beautiful strips....And then calm." No dream of "fear of the phallus," this is instead a dream of "fear of male power" under the aegis of which the institution of motherhood has been socially constructed and perpetuated. "To divide this power was sufficient to displace the fear" (268), to allow her to begin to reconstruct her familial relationships outside the "ready-made imagination" of the family as it has been socially constructed (268-69).[19] Thinking through her maternal body's experience, she arrives at a new politics of the family. At the personal level, this new understanding is one of the indices that her analysis is nearly over, and the Thing relegated to a small and contained corner in her psyche. At the level of gender politics in society, the text's final, single-sentence chapter— "May 1968 began a few days later"—offers this new politics of the family as not only a reconstruction of the social institution of motherhood, but also as the first step in a reconstruction of the state and of society in terms that made a place for women and for mothers.[20] For, if "what it meant to be a woman was to have a vagina," and, therefore, to engage in the repetitive, exhausting, and fraught work of mothering, what it meant to be a mother, was "absolute submission" in a society which permitted women and mothers "no role...other than to produce sons to carry on wars and found governments, and daughters who, in their turn, would produce sons" (264). To share power within the family, Cardinal's narrator concludes, is "the easiest way to begin" to share power in society (268). For readers such as Françoise Lionnet, who has traced the political implications of the identification of Algeria as the narrator's "real mother" and of the onset of the serious phase of her illness with her recognition that "we were about to assassinate Algeria" (88), this new politics of the family promises an end to "the cycle of war and exploitation" (1989: 202) that has been Algerian history. Cardinal's narrator does not venture beyond what she might achieve through her new familial relations; however, implicit in her recognition and her aims, as in her ending with May 1968, is the utopian possibility out-lined several years later by the philosopher Sara Ruddick: the possibility that rethinking the family might "transform maternal practice into a work of peace" (Ruddick 1989: 222).

Cardinal's autobiography remains unusual in that it represents not just giv-ing birth, but the experience of mothering, the institution of motherhood, a mother's ambivalent and fluctuating power within the family and her invisibility and powerlessness in society, as felt *corporeally*. That experience includes a mother's attentiveness to the physical presence of the child in her womb, with whom she lives in the greatest "intimacy or promiscuity" (Cardinal 1983: 139), the "tug right down to the genitals" which some mothers experience hold-ing a newborn next to their bodies or nursing (Gould 1988: 208), the desire to kiss and lick a newborn (222), and the physical tug of tenderness the sight of children's bodies not yet forced into self-conscious movement can arouse. These are pleasures only glancingly, if at all, represented in autobiography. It also includes the many kinds of *confinement* represented, many of them for the first time, by the poet alta, in her *momma: a start on all the untold stories* (1974). The confinement to bed to prevent miscarriages. The stopping up of words inside her as she tries not to make the old, old choice between living and writing a mother's stories, her "belly twisting w pain" before the conflict (74). The con-finement to her house, day in day out, trying to contain her frustrated desire for her husband's love so that it does not turn to physical rage against her daugh-ter: "this is unbearable. how can i write it. no wonder it is not written....no one could relate to such constant pain except another mother wishing to treat her children well" (10).

Still, and despite anomalous autobiographical moments such as these, a survey of representations of mothers' bodies in autobiography attests above all to the effectiveness of the suppression of those bodies within an institution of motherhood paradoxically grounded on them. We get glimpses of mothers' bodies in brief detours from the main direction of autobiographical narrative, in their displacements onto photographs or scholarly analysis, as somatic signs of psychic malignancy or of healthy new growth in the production of mothering. We don't see these bodies whole nor do they occupy the foreground of the scene; instead they are so overwritten by social inscriptions as to be nearly effaced *as* flesh. In short, they are bodies enmeshed in a social construction of motherhood which denies their very existence.

Above all, these autobiographies are strongly marked by their authors' pain. We cannot say, of course, the extent to which such pain may itself be socially and retrospectively produced by narratives such as those of psycho-analysis or the idealization of motherhood at least as much as by a specific mothering and a specific childhood. This may be particularly the case insofar as our cultural narratives, such as psychoanalytic theory or the many self-help-to-perfect-mothering guides, act as enforcers of social ideology at least as much as they act as explanatory models of psychic development. Given such factors, it is children, as we have seen, who will—occasionally—speak in autobiography about mothers' bodies, for the ideology and the narratives are child-centered. Daughters will speak with the greatest ambivalence, for it is daughters who are caught in the contradictory position of identifying with while separating from their mothers' bodies. And mothers will speak most tentatively, most evasively, of their own persons, their own bodies, because the narrative of motherhood has been founded on the non-representation of their persons, their bodies, and what goes unrepresented in culture is difficult to recognize as one's own experience. The fact that the autobiographies I have discussed are all recent—most were published during the last fifteen years—suggests that daughters and mothers and even an occasional son are making some small rents in the veil dropped over the experience of motherhood and that they are beginning to look on mothering and its reproduction as an experience lived through the body in ways at painful odds with its social construction.

But for all that, Jocasta has not yet spoken. We do not know why she desires her son, if indeed she *does* desire him outside the confines of psycho-analytic narrative, nor do we know what else she desires, feels, thinks, through her mothering body. Which is to say: we do not know what—as Adrienne Rich puts it in *Of Woman Born* (1976), the "cognitive potentiality" of bringing the mental and emotional capacities of mothering together with its physical experience might be. The autobiographies I have spoken about, however, suggest that we need to begin to think outside the cultural constructions of motherhood which psychoanalytic theories document and describe but need not circumscribe. They intimate that, if mother is named Jocasta, we had better learn about *all* her desires and her experiences of her body. They offer the possibility that mother thinks Jocasta a ridiculously exotic myth or merely a pretentious name and answers herself to the name and the life of a Sue or a Jill. And they remind us that we have only barely begun to heed Adrienne Rich's call to rethink motherhood by beginning to "*think through the body*" (284) so as to reconfigure and make visible the body that self-representation, in our culture, has depended upon effacing..

Notes

1   For a discussion of the emphasis on *production* in reproduction, beginning
    with industrialization, and resisted by the doctrines of Romanticism, see
    Andrea Henderson (1991). She argues that one result of this emphasis is an
    anxiety about the mother's ownership, or control over, her child "product."
    That anxiety leads de Sade to "'sew up the mother'" in the final scene of
    Philosophy in the Bedroom. It also "lends credibility" to Kristeva's concept of
    abjection: "that which 'preserves what existed in the archaism of pre-
    objectal relationship, in the immemorial *violence* with which a body becomes
    separated from another body in order to be'" (1984: 110-111)

2   A point made by many feminist theorists, but made early and notably by
    Gayle Rubin in "The Traffic in Women" (1975).

3   Kahn (1985: 74) and Suleiman (1985) both make the point that psycho-
    analytic theory is structured so as to make the child "the only self worth wor-
    rying about in the mother-child relationship" (Suleiman 356).

4   At first glance this conclusion would seem to be contradicted by the strong
    painterly tradition representing the Madonna and Child. In that tradition,
    however, the Madonna's focus, and therefore the viewer's, is on the Child.
    And, however many artists' mistresses served as models for the Madonna,
    however sensuously they are depicted, they are represented as unaware of
    their beauty; that is, their unawareness of their physical beauty represents
    their spiritual self-abnegation before the Son and is, in fact, a sign of their
    decorporealization. Telling here is the fact that, in a literary, painterly and reli-
    gious tradition which can and does represent the Immaculate Conception,
    the pregnant Mary, Mary suckling her newborn, and the grieving Mary of the
    Pietàs, Mary's labour of giving birth—the event in the narrative that most
    definitively points to her mothering flesh rather than to what Sara Ruddick
    (1989) calls "maternal thinking"—remains unspoken, unwritten, and invis-
    ible.

5   Margaret Homans summarizes: "The daughter therefore speaks two languages
    at once. Along with the symbolic language, she retains the literal or presym-
    bolic language that the son represses at the time of his renunciation of his
    mother. Just as there is for the daughter no oedipal 'crisis,' her entry into the
    symbolic order is only a gradual shift of emphasis" (1986: 13).

6   All psychoanalytic theory begins with the child's physical relation with the mother; it is the need to identify his body/his self as separate from his mother's that is the beginning of the child's identity-formation. What begins in these theories as a relationship in which the physical and emotional are indistinguishable in the psychic life, is then shown developing in terms that make the physical a figure of speech for the emotional life (as in the "castration" complex), but that, in fact, largely efface the lived (in) bodies of any actual child and his mother.

7   At its most extreme, this leads to the misogyny documented by Klaus Theweleit (1987-9) in the literature by and about members of the Freikorps in which the mother—and by extension, women—represent all that is fluid and potentially overwhelming, and in which male heroes, to avoid succumbing to this desired and feared reunion with their mothers' bodies, mutilate and kill wormen.

8   The implications of Leiris' autobiography for the construction of masculinity have been more fully elaborated by Peter Schwenger (1984) and, elsewhere, by myself (1991).

9   An ambivalence about Chitty's relation to her mother's body becomes evident if one compares this passage to one in an interview given E. Jane Dickson in which she says of her mother, "Physically there was something very lovable about her—she had a certain beauty and style and always had a nice personal smell—the kind of smell that gives you a feeling in the back of your throat, but she was not the kind of person you could run up to and hug" (1991: 17). However, in this and other interviews which were part of the publicity surrounding the publication of *Antonia White Diaries, 1926-1957 Volume I*, ed. Susan Chitty (London: Constable, 1991), Chitty also refers to hers and her sister's plans, as children, to murder their mother (see interviews with Dickson (1991) and de Courcy (1991)).

10 That Lizzie-cum-Hagar is about to enter the wilderness of death is emphasized by the dream's echo of the second epigraph to *Because I Was Flesh*: "'Why weepest thou, Hagar? Arise, take the child, and hold him in thine hand; for God hath heard thy voice and hath seen the child.' And she opened her eyes, and she saw a well of water, and she went and filled her bottle with water, and she gave the child to drink... .'"

11 On masculinity and gender in *Because I Was Flesh*, see Roger Porter (1991) and my "Autobiography and Manhood" (Neuman 1991).

12 Dahlberg imagines numerous conversations between Lizzie and possible suit-
   ors at which he could not have been present. He presents them in an
   overblown language of false sentiment and "respectability" hiding, but also
   betraying, a struggle for self-advantage. The rhetoric is a very literary version
   of an uneducated person's attempts at high-falutin' expression and, given to
   Lizzie by another, is very patronizing.

13 The New Look was long, with a high narrow waist from which large pleats,
   which got wider as they descended, fell. It was a fashion that marked
   social class through conspicuous consumption; coming as it did after the
   short straight skirts of the Second World War, and at a time when fabric was
   still in short supply and expensive, it became an index of affluence.

14 Steedman is countering here, with the specificity of "place and politics" in her
   own childhood, "the iconography of working-class motherhood that Jeremy
   Seabrook presents in *Working Class Childhood*" (6).

15 Cardinal sub-titles *The Words to Say It* as *A Novel*. Her next work, largely an
   interview with Annie Leclerc titled *Autrement Dit*, makes plain that the
   term "novel" is meant to distinguish this work from a document of psychoanalysis. That is, it is not a daily record of analysis, but rather written in
   retrospect; "So parts of my psychoanalysis have disappeared from it and others have expanded" (29). The autobiography in the work is never in question: "I have lived everything that the woman in the book lives" (29).

   Here the lines between literal referentiality and fictional "self-invention"—what Derrida terms the "life or ... body, if you will" and "the corpus
   called ...'s works" (1985: 44), become indistinguishable, but no more so than
   in most autobiographies. Cardinal speaks explicitly about the nexus of
   psychoanalysis, autobiography and self-invention in *The Words to Say It* when
   describing the story of her mother's story of her unsuccessful attempts to
   abort:

   > it didn't have a great importance in my analysis because I had a very pre-
   > cise memory of it and I had pulled from it all the conclusions possible
   > before beginning treatment....But, in writing it, it became enormous....In
   > writing it, I became aware that this story corresponded to all the defeated
   > women of the world, it was even stronger, it made most visible the
   > abandonment/evacuation* of the little girl. I was already far from the truth,
   > and nonetheless I was in the middle of it. When I write, I always depart
   > from something... I have lived, and then that transforms itself, opens up,
   > divagates, the "I" can become a "she," but "she" is I even more than "I" am.

(1977: 30)

*[The French phrase here is "le rejet de la petite fille," which carries both the sense of "abandon" and the slang expression "rejet"—or turd—for a baby.]

[16] Marguerite Le Clézio notes that "The mother's body, and the land, Algeria, are metaphorically conjoined as symbols of origins from which the daughter is drastically severed" (1981: 385); Colette Hall follows suit with her observation that, in Cardinal's earlier fiction, both the sea and Algeria "work as metonymic representations of the mother" (1988: 235). The imagery of mutilation, as well as that of blood, however, also suggest that Cardinal *herself* identifies with, and is alienated from, Algeria just as her pregnancies, at the same time as they make her mother "revolting" to her (1983: 138), will cause her to reproduce her mother's desire for abortion in her somatic production of the blood that her mother's strenuous efforts had failed to make appear. Among Cardinal's critics, Françoise Lionnet most fully explores what she calls the "conflation of maternal body and country of origin" (1989: 205). Lionnet sees the mother as "like Algeria during the war of independence," her "agony... the scene of a civil war between conflicting ideologies" (199); at the same time, she argues, "only hysteria," such as that the narrator manifests in her ambivalent identification with her mother/Algeria, "can transform the dominant codes through and by which we become self-aware as a collective body-politic" (24).

[17] Patricia Elliot, reading "the Thing" in terms of Kristeva's theory of abjection, notes that it is precisely "the failure to repress the fantasy of fusion with the mother" (1987: 74), a fantasy first of desire, then, after her mother's revelations, of loathing, that leads to the projection of anxiety onto "the Thing." The recognition of her mother as a subject separate from her marks the end of that fantasy.

[18] This analogy of child and feces operates quite differently than such comparisons as used by, for example, de Sade or Freud. De Sade "effaces the laborious aspect of childbearing by comparing it to growing fingernails and defecating, considering all three as forms of 'emanation'" (Henderson, 1991: 110). In Freudian theory the feces symbolize the baby as product. It is this understanding that informs Marie Cardinal's self-denigrating rage when, in the middle of her Freudian analysis, she describes her own unwanted birth: "At the last, powerless, resigned, defeated, disappointed, she let me slip out alive into life, the way you let slip a turd. And what about that little girl/turd coming slowly...?" (1983: 140). Gould's analogy works in an

opposite way: the "product" is incidental; what is significant is the effort, the labour, to expel it.

[19] That women do not wish to become men, or to possess a penis "for its own sake," but that they do want the power to which men have access in our society and which the penis has come to symbolize, is a point also made in feminist revisions of psychoanalytic theory. See, for example, Chodorow's discussion, in *The Reproduction of Mothering* (1979: 123-24), of Janine Chassenguet-Smirgel's "Feminine Guilt and the Oedipus Complex," in *Female Sexuality*, ed. Janine Chassenguet-Smirgel (Ann Arbor: University of Michigan P, 1970): 94-134.

[20] This chapter is suppressed in the English translation. Elaine Martin (1981) points to its social significance (45); Françoise Lionnet points to the utopian connection of "the revolutionary potential of psychoanalysis" with "political emancipation" (1989: 206).

Works Cited

alta. (1974). *Momma: a start on all the untold stories*. New York: Times Change Press.

Barthes, Roland. (1981). *Camera Lucida: Reflections on Photography*. Trans. Richard Howard. New York: Hill and Wang. (1980). *La Chambre claire*. Paris: Seuil.

Cardinal, Marie. (1977). *Autrement dit*. Paris: Grasset.[my trans.]

———.(1983). *The Words to Say It*. Trans. Pat Goodheart. Cambridge, MA: VanVactor and Goodheart. (1975). *Les Mots pour le dire*. Paris: Grasset et Fasquelle.

Carrighar, Sally. (1973). *Home to the Wilderness*. Boston: Houghton Mifflin.

Chernin, Kim. (1983). *In My Mother's House*. New York: Harper and Row.

Chitty, Susan. (1985). *Now to My Mother: A Very Personal Memoir of Antonia White*. London: Weidenfeld and Nicholson.

Chodorow, Nancy. (1980). "Gender, Relation, and Difference in Psychoanalytic Perspective," *The Future of Difference*. Ed. Hester Eisenstein and Alice Jardine, 3-19. Boston: G.K. Hall.

———.(1979). *The Reproduction of Mothering: Psychoanalysis and the Sociology of Gender*. Berkeley: University of California Press.

Clézio, Marguerite Le. (1981). "Mother and Motherland: The Daughter's Quest for Origins," *Stanford French Review* 5.3: 381-89.

Conway, Jill Ker. (1989). *The Road from Coorain*. New York: Knopf.

Dahlberg, Edward. (1959). *Because I Was Flesh: The Autobiography of Edward Dahlberg*. New York: New Directions.

de Courcy, Anne. (1991). "'We planned to murder Mother with a cook's knife'" [interview with Susan Chitty]. *Evening Standard* (16 August): 17.

Derrida, Jacques. (1985). *The Ear of the Other: Otobiography, Transference, Translation*. Ed. Christie V. McDonald. Trans. Peggy Kamuf. New York: Schocken. (1982). *L'Oreille de l'autre*. Ed. Claude Lévesque and Christie V. McDonald. Montréal: VLB.

Dickson, E. Jane. (1991). "Swearing on Her Mother's Grave" [Interview with Susan Chitty]. *The Times Saturday Review* (31 August): 16-17.

Elliot, Patricia. (1987). "In the Eye of Abjection: Marie Cardinal's *The Words to Say It*." *Mosaic* 20.4 (Fall): 71-81.

Freud, Sigmund. (1966). *The Complete Introductory Lectures on Psychoanalysis*. Trans. and ed. James Strachey. New York: Norton.

Gagnier, Regenia. (1989). "The Literary Standard, Working-Class Lifewriting, and Gender." *Textual Practice* 3.1 (Spring): 36-55.

Gould, Joan. (1988). *Spirals: A Woman's Journey Through Family Life*. (1989). New York, London: Penguin.

Hall, Colette. (1988). "*L'Ecriture féminine* and the Search for the Mother in the Works of Violette Leduc and Marie Cardinal," *Women in French Literature*. Ed. Michel Guggenheim, 231-38. California: Anma Libri.

Henderson, Andrea. (1991). "Doll-Machines and Butcher-Shop Meat: Models of Childbirth in the Early Stages of Industrial Capitalism," *Genders* 12 (Winter): 100-119.

Hirsch, Marianne. (1989). *The Mother/Daughter Plot: Narrative, Psychoanalysis, Feminism*. Bloomington: Indiana University Press.

Homans, Margaret. (1986). *Bearing the Word: Language and Female Experience in Nineteenth-Century Women's Writing*. Chicago: University of Chicago Press.

Irigaray, Luce. (1981). *Le corps-à-corps avec la mère*. Montréal: Les éditions de la pleine lune. [my trans.]

Kahn, Coppélia. (1985). "The Hand That Rocks the Cradle: Recent Gender Theories and Their Implications," *The (M)other Tongue: Essays in Feminist Psychoanalytic Interpretation*. Eds. Shirley Nelson Garner, Claire Kahane and Madelon Sprengnether, 72-88. Ithaca, London: Cornell University Press.

Kristeva, Julia. (1984). *Revolution in Poetic Language*. Trans. Margaret Walker. New York: Columbia University Press.

Lacan, Jacques. (1982). *Feminine Sexuality: Jacques Lacan and the "école freudienne*," Eds. Juliet Mitchell and Jacqueline Rose. Trans. Jacqueline Rose. New York, London: Norton.

——.(1977). "The mirror stage as formative of the function of the I as revealed in psychoanalytic experience," *Écrits: A Selection*, 1-7. Trans. Alan Sheridan. New York: Norton.

Lehmann, Rosamond. (1967). *The Swan in the Evening: Fragments of an Inner Life.* Rev. (1982). London: Virago.

Leiris, Michel. (1984). *Manhood: A Journey from Childhood into the Fierce Order of Virility.* Trans. Richard Howard. San Francisco: North Point Press. (1939, Rev. 1946, 1973). *L'Age d'homme.* Paris: Gallimard.

Lévi-Strauss, Claude. (1969). *The Elementary Structures of Kinship.* Trans. James Harle Bell, John Richard Von Sturmer and Rodney Needham. Rev. London: Eyre and Spottiswode. (1949, 1968). *Les Structures élémentaires de la parenté.* Paris: Mouton.

Lionnet, Françoise. (1989). *Autobiographical Voices: Race, Gender, Self-Portraiture.* Ithaca: Cornell University Press.

Martin, Elaine. (1981). "Mothers, Madness, and the Middle Class in *The Bell Jar* and *Les Mots pour le dire*," *The French-American Review* 5.1 (Spring): 24-47.

Nabokov, Vladimir. (1966). *Speak, Memory: An Autobiography Revisited.* (1970). New York: Capricorn.

Neuman, Shirley. (1991). "Autobiography, Bodies, Manhood," *Autobiography and Questions of Gender.* Ed. Shirley Neuman. *Prose Studies* 14.2 (Sept): 137-65. (1992). London: Frank Cass.

Olivier, Christiane. (1989). *Jocasta's Children: The Imprint of the Mother.* Trans. George Craig. London, New York: Routledge. (1980). *Enfants de Jocaste.* Paris: Editions Denoël.

Porter, Roger J. (1991). "Figuration and Disfigurement: Herculine Barbin and the Autobiography of the Body," *Autobiography and Questions of Gender.* Ed. Shirley Neuman. *Prose Studies* 14.2 (Sept): 122-36. (1992). London: Frank Cass.

Reimer, Gail Twersky. (1988). "Revisions of Labor in Margaret Oliphant's Autobiography," *Life/Lines: Theorizing Women's Autobiography.* Eds. Bella Brodzki and Celeste Schenck, 203-20. Ithaca, London: Cornell University Press.

Rich, Adrienne. (1976). *Of Woman Born: Motherhood as Experience and Institution.* New York, London: Norton.

Roy, Gabrielle. (1987). *Enchantment and Sorrow: The Autobiography of Gabrielle Roy.* Trans. Patricia Claxton. Toronto: Lester and Orpen Dennys. (1984). *La Détresse et l'enchantement.* Montréal: Boréal.

Rubin, Gayle. (1975). "The Traffic in Women: Notes on the 'Political Economy' of Sex," *Toward an Anthropology of Women*. Ed. Rayna R. Reiter, 157-210. New York: Monthly Review Press.

Ruddick, Sara. (1989). *Maternal Thinking: Toward a Politics of Peace*. New York: Ballantine.

Schwenger, Peter. (1984). *Phallic Critiques: Masculinity and Twentieth-Century Literature*. London: Routledge and Kegan Paul.

Steedman, Carolyn Kay. (1986). *Landscape for a Good Woman: A Story of Two Lives*. London: Virago.

Suleiman, Susan Rubin. (1985). "Writing and Motherhood," *The (M)other Tongue: Essays in Feminist Psychoanalytic Interpretation*. Eds. Shirley Neslon Garner, Claire Kahane and Madelon Sprengnether, 352-77. Ithaca, London: Cornell University Press.

Theweleit, Klaus. (1987-9). *Male Fantasies*. 2 Vols. Trans. Stephen Conway, Erica Carter and Chris Turner. Minneapolis: University of Minnesota Press.

Index

MARQUIS
Montmagny, Qc